HUBERT HOWARD

❧

A Man for
All Seasons

'His greatness of spirit, his true nobility, his immense
generosity, his courage and his strength and his gentleness
all combined to make him one of the very greatest of men.'

THETIS BLACKER

Hubert Howard on the summit of Monte Semprevisa, April 1978

HUBERT HOWARD

A Man for All Seasons

A biographical tribute by

ESME HOWARD

Foreword by the Duke of Norfolk

MARBLE HILL ✠ LONDON

First published in 2021 by
Marble Hill Publishers
Flat 58 Macready House
75 Crawford Street
London W1H 5LP
www.marblehillpublishers.co.uk

A CIP catalogue record for this book is
available from the British Library.

ISBN 978-1-8383036-4-8

Typeset in 11.5pt/15pt Adobe Jenson Pro,
with chapter titles set in ITC Golden Type
and drop caps in Charlemagne. Cover fonts
are Albertus, Bodoni and Calvert.

Printed and bound in the UK by Biddles Books

Book design by Dan Brown

Contents

*In memory of Hubert and Lelia,
with admiration, gratitude
and affection.*

Foreword

As a founder member of the International Friends of Ninfa, I am well aware of my kinsman Hubert Howard's devotion to the Caetani family and his pivotal role in securing their unique cultural patrimony. The world-famous garden of Ninfa, in particular, which I first experienced in 1994 during a visit to Rome to honour the two Howard cardinals, is uniquely inspiring.

Hubert's life was shaped by extraordinary circumstances, and, not unlike the history of the Howards, it had its unexpected turns. His own quiet modesty could easily have had the effect of denying us the richness of his experiences and of his many accomplishments. Esme Howard's biographical tribute, marking the fiftieth anniversary of one of the several Caetani foundations which Hubert was instrumental in founding, is a timely, intimate and captivating glimpse into Hubert's life and times. It will ensure, rightly, that he will remain alive in our memories.

Edward Norfolk

THE DUKE OF NORFOLK

Acknowledgements

My first thanks go to the Roffredo Caetani Foundation for having suggested I write this biography and for having done so much, over many years and in different ways, to honour and celebrate Hubert's life. In this connection, I am grateful to Arch. Tommaso Agnoni, chairman, and Dr Giovanni Pesiri, councillor. It is planned that this English edition will be followed in 2022 by one in Italian, also by way of celebrating the foundation's fiftieth anniversary.

I am grateful to His Grace the Duke of Norfolk for his foreword to this book, and for permission to use several images from the Arundel archives. Special thanks go to John Martin Robinson, librarian to the duke, and to Craig Irving, archivist.

The Maria Sofia Giustiniani Bandini Foundation in Camerino, its chairman Avv. Luigi Tapanelli and archivist Lorenzo Capenti, have also generously allowed me the use of several images.

I especially wish to thank those of Hubert's Italian friends who have been able to share their memories with me, in particular Clotilde Luchetti, Lauro Marchetti, Benedetta Origo and Fulco Pratesi.

Others who have helped me in a variety of ways include: Laura Baldeschi, Marella Caracciolo Chia, Paola Cerocchi, Caterina Fiorani, Florence Hammond, Grevel Lindop, Adam Munthe, Federica Nardacci, Charles Quest-Ritson and The Society of The Work at Littlemore.

Closer to home, I am indebted to those family members who have provided me with private documents and photographs, information, memories and much else. Among these are my daughter Elizabeth Dunhill, my son Edmund Howard, my brothers John and Anthony Howard, and my cousins Philip Howard, Joan Howard, Henry Howard and Esme Lowe.

Particular thanks go to two author friends, Gay Daly and Laurie Dennett, who gave me wise guidance from differing perspectives and from different continents. For so much help with PWB research, and the war in Italy, I am most grateful to Dr Gervase Vernon.

In terms of quotations and illustrative materials for this book, I have done everything within my power to seek all the necessary copyright permissions. I apologise if I have missed anything and if so the failure is mine alone.

It has been a joy to have published with Marble Hill, where Francis Bennett has given me the advantage of clear views and many years of professional experience. Dan Brown's elegant and imaginative design, and his attention to detail, have enriched the book in so many ways. I thank too my niece Isabella Woods for her editorial input, and her considerable patience with my texts.

Wives so often come last in being acknowledged by their writer-husbands. Diane's contribution to the entire process of writing and nurturing this book cannot be overstated. Always with good grace, she helped me make the most of an unusually unencumbered diary during the many months of the Covid-19 pandemic.

It is fitting, in conclusion, to thank the members of that great circle of Hubert's departed friends and family whose letters, tributes and memories of him have been crucial to the writing of this biography.

Introduction

It has not been simple to uncover and then condense into one short volume the events, contours, colours and direction of Hubert Howard's richly variegated life. Hubert was an intensely private man, and might even have disapproved of the notion of a biography. In a letter to me, dated 13 September 1986, when already he knew he was dying, he wrote:

> I never seem to do very much, nor very successfully, nor can I express myself fortunately as other people are gifted to do. But what I do get are wonderful letters from friends, which give me everything I can wish for in life. In fact, 'letters from friends' would make my best biography, and only justification.

We should resist, even posthumously, Hubert's natural tendency to downplay his life's work. As I researched his life, I realised that he was very much 'a man for all seasons': one who coped with what life flung at him, and did so with grace and courage. He weathered many storms, and even put himself in harm's way to be of help to others. One is struck by how he handled not only the adversity that came his way but also the decidedly mixed blessings of having been born to privilege. The concluding phase of his life, as an 'adoptive' son of the Caetani and married to a person whom he adored, is the stuff of fable but was not without some harsh challenges.

As a nephew and godson, I knew Hubert for forty-nine years of my life, counting myself among those, still living, who miss him as one would a close friend. His kindly presence in this complicated world was not only reassuring to all who knew him but also a blessing. When I think of Hubert, I think of a humble person, little affected by the aristocratic privilege into which he was born: on his father's side a member of one of the oldest families of the English nobility, and, on his mother's, a descendant of one of the old Venetian Republic's most notable families. He enjoyed a close and stable family life, a fine education and a wide array of friendships. Through his parents' connections, his life might well have fallen into a predictable career pattern. It is all the richer, perhaps, for not having done so.

As the son of a diplomat, Hubert travelled widely. After university, he was unsure about which career to pursue. For a while, before and during World War II, he contemplated (as he did the priesthood) the quasi-hermitic life of a farmer in his beloved Cumbria, where his father had been born and which has so many associations with our branch of the Howards. Instead, as soon as his wartime adventures were over, and through a series of coincidences, he met and fell in love with Lelia Caetani. This was his epiphany – the moment, almost exactly halfway through his life, when he changed course forever. He became a devoted husband, sharing with Lelia the joys and challenges of stewarding and protecting the unique Caetani patrimony in Rome and in the Terra Pontina, and espousing the cause of conservational heritage more generally in Italy. Hubert and Lelia enjoyed not quite twenty-six years together before her untimely death in 1977. In his remaining years, Hubert's devotion to her family never lessened.

I have tried in this short biography first to uncover, with due sensitivity, the essence of Hubert's character and personality, and the family and spiritual influences on his life; second, to introduce the Giustiniani Bandini family from whom he was descended on his mother's side, and to trace the rich Anglo-Italian complementarity between the historic Howards and Caetani; and, third, to delve deeper into the conservational and cultural passions which Hubert shared and expressed with Lelia in so many generous, valuable and lasting ways. I write with a certain nostalgia as one who lived when the presence of the Caetani was still a reality and who, through my subsequent work with Lelia's foundations, has experienced inevitable changes.

There is a considerable bibliography in terms of the Howard and Caetani families, and much invaluable material in the archives and among the publications of the Caetani foundations. That it has been possible to trace Hubert's life prior to his marriage to Lelia, however, is owed largely to Hubert's diaries, reports, and correspondence, the bulk of which resides in the Howard family archives, some materials discovered only recently.

It became clear to me that my late father Edmund, to whom I refer throughout by his nickname of 'Mondi', had contemplated writing a biography of his brother Hubert. Among the family papers are his copious handwritten notes, setting out Hubert's life and quoting from his many letters and reports. These notes were an invaluable source of material for this book.

On his last visit to England in September 1986, and having put his affairs in order at his home in Cumbria, Hubert came to stay with me in London for a few days. During this time, he revealed with selfless composure the shocking reality that due to the onset of cancer he had only a few months to live. His death, on 17 February 1987, was followed by an outpouring of affection in so very many letters and personal tributes. I have to admit that none of this surprised me, and I feel particularly honoured to have been given the task of writing about him.

ESME HOWARD
The Gallery House
October 2021

CHAPTER ONE

The Tower by the Lake

I T may seem improbable that Hubert John Edward Dominic Howard, exemplar of Anglo-Italian descent, should have been born at 2208 Massachusetts Avenue, in Washington. The explanation is that his father, Esme Howard, was on the first of two diplomatic postings to the capital, this one as chargé d'affaires at the British Embassy.[1] The date was 23 December 1907 and the incumbent American president was Theodore Roosevelt, with whose family Esme and his sons were to become friends. Whereas Roosevelt's nickname, Teddy, derived from a bear cub captured on one of the president's hunting trips, not unnaturally Hubert's Italian mother, Isabella, immediately nicknamed the baby boy 'Bimbo', although in later life, more suitably, his family resorted to the diminutive, 'Hubie'. Sadly, there are few accounts of Hubert in his childhood. We know, however, that the brothers, cloistered together in a succession of diplomatic residences, teased one another as siblings often do, and that this continued in the most affectionate way even into adulthood.

Notwithstanding his Italian heritage, or the fact that he had spoken Italian with his mother from an early age and went on to live many years in Italy, Hubert was nonetheless perceived by his Italian friends as quintessentially far more English than Italian – in his bearing, manner, and way of thinking. In a moving and affectionate tribute to him, soon after his death, the distinguished conservationist Bonaldo Stringher,[2] friend and colleague, observed that Hubert 'almost deliberately' allowed traces of his English pronunciation to show through in his spoken Italian, just as he occasionally muddled his syntax and grammar. As if to bear this out, the late Avv. Giacomo Antonelli, who worked alongside him for many years, remembered how Hubert would use the non-existent *soprasotto* when meaning *sottosopra* (upside down). He also recalled Hubert's occasional Anglo-Saxon stubbornness – or *spigolosità* – which would surface from time to time in his way of arguing, the more so when insistent or mildly irritated about points of fact or principle; and, when it came to principle, Hubert was almost too honest for his own good, recoiling on one occasion from participating in a game of Liar Dice with his English nephews and nieces.

Temperamentally, Hubert differed from his four brothers: Esme or 'Esmetto', and Francis, both older than he; and his two younger ones, Edmund or 'Mondi', and Henry.[3] (For the sake of clarity, throughout this

The five Howard brothers: (left to right) Mondi, Francis, Esmetto, Henry and Hubert, Stockholm, *c.* 1914

2

book Esme will be referred to as 'Esmetto' and Edmund as 'Mondi'.) In certain ways Hubert was more reserved than his siblings and, as he grew older, he became ever more attentive to detail, scrupulously punctual and polite, and charmingly fussy. In one letter to his parents, while at Cambridge University, he described himself as 'naturally pessimistic'. Indeed, there had always been an affectionate family speculation that Hubert, with his furrowed brow, was born worried.

On an unseasonably cold day in May 1972, Hubert and his wife Lelia lunched at Alderley Grange in Gloucestershire as guests of James and Alvilde Lees-Milne.[4] Hubert admired Lees-Milne's prominent work at the National Trust, and over time had entertained them both at Ninfa. In his diaries (*A Mingled Measure: Diaries 1953–1972*) Lees-Milne describes Hubert as 'a man of wide interests, culture and reading ... [having] a correct sense of humour ... [and being] easy to talk to and full of charm ... Quiet, gentle, very patrician'. In the same breath, so to speak, he cannot resist writing these words:

> But these old Catholic families always put me on my guard, for with all their seeming tolerance and gentle mockery of others of their persuasion, they are underneath *très dévots*, and nothing, nothing will allow them for one minute to let you think they are the same as the majority of mankind. They have a subtle, inner arrogance, which will rise to the surface with a scratch.

Lees-Milne was born Protestant, but became for a period in his life what one might term a 'fashionable' Catholic. At about the time of the Alderney lunch, he was becoming increasingly disillusioned with what he perceived as the 'travesty' of the reformed Mass of Vatican II. He probably provoked Hubert with a remark, for he seeks here to depict Hubert as one whose immovable faith creates in him the delusion that he is in some way set apart. One is reminded of John Henry Newman's famous *Apologia Pro Vita Sua* written in response to a similar kind of provocation – with the added sting that he (Newman) did not really believe the 'unbelievable' tenets of Roman Catholicism.[5]

There are certainly Catholics such as the diarist describes, some indeed born of old aristocratic, recusant and traditionalist families, some shaped by the Council of Trent and as submissive to the orthodoxies and practices of the old faith as they are dismissive of Vatican II. The diarist, however, had entirely misunderstood Hubert, who never knowingly set himself apart from others. Having an eclectic sense of humour, and being self-deprecating and instinctively unassertive, Hubert was in no danger of becoming pedantic or pompous. To those who knew him well he was the refreshing antithesis of hubris, self-aggrandisement and selfishness. Privileged he may have been, but without any sense of entitlement. Exactly like his father, he made discreet fun of the rituals and posturing of wealth, social status and power. He always championed the poor and the underprivileged and, were he alive today, he would have disliked the millennial fixation with 'celebrities' and the wastefulness and banality of so much of social media.

As to the tenets of Roman Catholicism, Hubert, unashamedly a man of the deep and devotional faith inherited from his mother, was almost scholarly in his knowledge and understanding of the history, ecclesiology and theology of the Church. He read the Bible and the Church Fathers avidly, understood the Reformation, accepted Vatican II on merit, and even entertained the notion of becoming a priest. In any case, Lees-Milne's observations of Hubert serve only at a social or superficial level. Far deeper than this, Hubert was subconsciously rooted in the three transcendentals of Truth, Beauty, and Goodness. He was profoundly innocent, keenly attuned to the marvels and beauty of nature as we see in his works of environmental conservation, and one who led by example and did much good in his lifetime. A man of his times, to be sure, but countercultural and in many ways prophetic.

This brief introductory portrait of Hubert needs family and formative context. Hubert's childhood, for the most part happy, involved moving to wherever his father's career took him, being dependent on tutors and governesses, and subject to the formality associated with the diplomatic life a hundred years ago. As it was for Hubert's brothers, such an upbringing offered advantages and disadvantages. By the time the boys finished boarding school in England, not only were they widely travelled, but they had also grown accustomed to the sights and sounds of different European languages and cultures, and were cosmopolitan and mature in their bearing. However, between 1903 (the year of Esmetto's birth) and 1918 (when World War I ended), the boys had had no opportunity to visit the beautiful Lake District, so beloved of their father. By then Hubert was ten years old and had lived in Washington, his birthplace; Budapest (where Mondi was born); Berne (where Henry was born); and, finally, Stockholm.

A SENSE of place is also key to our understanding of Hubert. That his earliest instincts turned towards nature and conservation can be traced to his father Esme's lifelong love of beauty and the wild, as well as devotion to the countryside of his birth: the Lake District, and particularly Ullswater. Esme wrote about these with passion in his autobiography *Theatre of Life*, describing them as 'the most precious jewel in the crown of England', and their defence against 'utilitarian' encroachment as vital.[6] Esme also loved wild birds and opposed their unnatural and cruel captivity as caged pets, such as he had once witnessed on a visit to San Gimignano in Italy. The same practices were widespread in England too. Soon after his retirement, he lobbied with others to bring about a law, the Bird Bill of 1933, banning the trade in wild birds. Such example was embedded in the young Hubert and was to prove a constant source of motivation.

The Lake District is the very heart of the county of Cumbria (formerly Cumberland and Westmorland), the third largest in the land. It lies in the northwest of England and is renowned for its mountains (or 'fells' as they are known locally), its sixteen deep and glacial lakes, magnificent walks and traditional inns. It is also noted for its early nineteenth-century 'Lake' Poets, among them William Wordsworth (who described Ullswater as the 'noblest of Lakes'), Samuel Taylor Coleridge and Robert Southey.[7] This area, today designated a World Heritage site, lies an hour's drive south of Scotland's southwestern border. In the summer season its narrow lanes

Greystoke Castle, Cumbria, birthplace of Hubert's father, Esme Howard

are overrun by tourists and day trippers. In autumn and winter, along with a great deal of rain, the winds come off the fells and plunge into the valleys to chilling effect. It can be very cold indeed in these parts, but for the amateur climber there is comfort in the knowledge that mountain rescue teams are always at the ready.

Greystoke Castle, one of several Howard castles in the county, lies close to the market town of Penrith. There, in September 1863, Hubert's father Esme was born, the youngest of six siblings. His parents were Henry Howard and Charlotte Long; his brothers Henry, Stafford and Mowbray; and his sisters Elizabeth (always known as 'Elsie') and Maud. The origins of the castle go back to the eleventh century when it was little more than a fortified tower and a stockade. Over time it was repeatedly strengthened to repel robbers and Scottish border incursions and, as a residence and an estate, it grew in grandeur. In Esme's time, the Greystoke estate extended to about 6,000 acres. At its peak, however, with all its outlying farms and lands, it was said to encompass at least 30,000 acres. Eighteen successive generations of the de Greystoke family lived there. It then passed in Elizabethan times to the Howards follow-ing 'auspicious' marriages between the three sons of Thomas Howard (1536–72), 4th Duke of Norfolk, and the three daughters of his third wife, Elizabeth, whose first husband's family, the Dacres of Gillesland, owned almost the entire county. As the de Greystoke owners were traditionally Catholics and Royalists, Oliver Cromwell's army of the north made a vicious and punitive attack on the castle in 1660, in the aftermath of the English Civil War. Very much later, in 1868, when Esme was four and present in the building, a maid left a lighted candle in a linen cupboard and a disastrous fire occurred, which he describes vividly in his memoir. The castle, as we see it today, was substantially redesigned following the fire.

Being a fourth son, Esme Howard did not inherit Greystoke Castle, but stayed there whenever he could during his life. With the permission of his eldest brother Henry, he also made increasing use of a rather curious property, part of the estate and situated some nine miles due southwest, overlooking Ullswater. Its name is Lyulph's Tower, often referred to as

Fire at Greystoke Castle, as reported in the *Illustrated London News*, 16 May 1868

Hubert's father, Esme Howard,
aged four, in a portrait by
Julia Margaret Cameron

'the Tower'. It has an extraordinary attraction, not so much as a house but because it commands the most perfectly elevated frontal view of the lake, with lush meadows reaching down to the lakeside, from whose pebbled shores one can admire mountain ranges and gain an occasional glimpse of Helvellyn, the third highest peak in Cumbria and in all of England. Behind the Tower the scenic fells of Gowbarrow Park rise steeply.

The property has an unusual history. The dukedom of Norfolk passed through the Greystoke line of Howards only once, and was handled to reasonably good effect by a father and son whose characters were entirely different: the first quiet, the second boisterous and unpredictable. They were the tenth and eleventh Dukes of Norfolk. The former, Charles Howard of Greystoke (1720–86), who inherited the family estates upon the death of his father, was retiring and eccentric. His passions were history, genealogy and gardening. Wine, it was said, seemed to be the only thing that brought him to life and enabled him to speak freely about his

Catholic faith. In his own words he was a 'Whig [liberal] papist, a monster in nature' and he had a tendency towards isolation and melancholia.[8]

His son, another Charles (1746–1815), succeeded him as eleventh duke. Although finely educated and reasonably travelled as a child of the Enlightenment, various descriptions tell of how different he was from his father and how 'unlike a Howard'. From a diarist of that time, 'Nature which cast him in her coarsest mould, had not bestowed on him any of the external insignia of high descent. His person large, muscular, and clumsy, was destitute of grace or dignity.' Charles may have been inelegant and rough in his manner, and somewhat addicted to claret, but he was a most generous patron of the arts and a fine amateur architect who did a great deal to restore Arundel Castle, in Sussex, the principal seat of the Dukes of Norfolk.[9]

The younger Charles very much loved Greystoke, and yet he craved some sort of retreat at the far end of the estate. In 1780 he built Lyulph's Tower, which he named after the Norman, Ligulf de Greystoke, who is said to have built the original stockade at Greystoke. This 'castellated folly', built in a neo-Gothic style, quickly became a landmark for all

Lyulph's Tower, Ullswater

those travelling the lakeside road from Pooley Bridge to Glenridding or observing it from the opposite side, where there is only a footpath. In 1799, Wordsworth and Coleridge made a walking tour of Ullswater. The former described seeing 'deep within the bosom of the lake, a magnificent castle, with towers and battlements'.[10] Coleridge was no less captivated:

> [As] the fog begins to clear off from the lake … and clings viscously to the hill, all the objects on the opposite coast are hidden, and all those hidden are reflected in the lake, trees, and the castle … and the huge cliff that dwarfs it! Divine! … Lyulph's Tower gleams like a ghost, dim and shadowy … [A moment later it] rises emerging out of the mist, two-thirds wholly hidden, the turrets quite clear; and [in] a moment all is snatched away – realities and shadows.[11]

Later, Wordsworth felt rather duped by his first impressions and apparently dismissed the Tower as a mere 'pleasure house', which was not the case although, in the eleventh duke's time, and since, it had been used for shooting parties, late-night drinking and some gambling. The building, which at a distance does give the impression of a grand hexagonal *castelletto* or fortified mansion, is actually a four-towered retaining wall with a house slung onto the back. It begs completion.

Just prior to the outbreak of World War II, Hubert acquired the Tower from his aunt Mabel Howard, widow of his eldest uncle, Henry. He paid £5,000 for the house and farm, in all about eighty acres. He was faced with a great deal of expense for repairs and maintenance, and he doggedly carried on with these works until his death. In his lifetime, Hubert planted many trees on the property, improved the outbuildings and did what he could with the sloping garden. He was active in Cumbrian conservation, and was generous in funding a small local Catholic chapel, named after St Philip Howard. Hubert's last visit to the Tower was in December 1986, two months before he died.[12]

CHAPTER TWO

Esme and Isabella

THE story of Hubert's parents is remarkable and casts a great deal of light on Hubert's life, his outlook, his habits and tastes, as well as his expectations. His father, Esme, had a profound sense of family and tradition. True, he was brought up as a member of the upper classes, moving during his holidays between Howard castles such as Greystoke and Thornbury, as well as Pixton and Highclere (homes of the Carnarvon Herberts who are cousins by marriage)[1] and Charlton Park, home of the Earl of Suffolk who was his uncle. Yet there was not a trace of snobbery or cliquishness in him. He mixed well and enjoyed riding and field sports. He inherited this, no doubt, from his father, Henry Howard of Greystoke, but his unpretentious mother was also curious about the world and keen to explore and experience it to the full.

At Harrow School, where Esme was sent at the age of thirteen, he made the most of his time there although his Latin teacher told him that he would never be more than 'a respectable mediocrity'. On leaving school in summer 1881, he adapted easily to spending the ensuing winter and spring in Florence with his mother and sister Maud. Esme put aside notions of university, which he later regretted, and opted immediately for a diplomatic career as if he knew his vocation. He completed his diplomatic exams in 1885, one of only four to pass in that year. He was twenty-one. His brother-in-law, Henry Herbert, 4th Earl of Carnarvon, was assigned to Dublin as Viceroy of Ireland soon after Esme joined the

Esme Howard as attaché in Rome, 1886

Foreign Office. Esme willingly accepted Henry's offer to join him there as his assistant private secretary, thus starting an experimental phase in his fledgling diplomatic career. In February 1886, Esme moved to the British Embassy in Rome where he worked for two years as an unpaid attaché, the 'scrub of the embassy' as he described it. Nevertheless, his brief time there put in motion a course of events that was to change his life profoundly. Socialising was part of the job, and Esme's eligibility and connections soon got him invitations to the most glittering balls and social events. Having first met and been attracted by a young lady at one such event, he asked his Roman friends about her and was reassured that, even if elusive, she was the sweetest person imaginable. Esme's courtship of her, an epic tale of patience and perseverance, was gently ignited during this period although socially impossible to reveal.

In 1888, he transferred to Berlin as the embassy's third secretary, and two years later opted out of diplomacy, concerned, as he put it, 'not to end up a specimen of dry, withered officialism by the time I am 65'. He took two years' leave of absence, starting in 1891, on a basis that would allow him to return to diplomacy without loss of position. He took his mother to South Africa, leaving her in Cape Town while he went with a few companions on an adventurous trek to the northern territories of Rhodesia, now part of Zimbabwe, with some notion of finding gold. In the election year, 1892, Esme now flirted impulsively with politics, standing against overwhelming odds as Liberal Home Rule candidate for Worcester. A year later, he made two trips to Morocco and, in ensuing travels, he went to Brazil to examine possibilities in the rubber industry. It seemed that Esme craved adventure and the world at that time made it plentifully available to him.

In spring of 1896, when he was thirty-two, Esme went back out to Rome with his mother, for her health, and also to see if he could at least attract the attention of that young woman to whom he felt so drawn. The full name of his 'heart's desire', as he referred to her, was Princess Maria Isabella Giovanna Teresa Gioacchina Giustiniani Bandini. Of that great litany of names, Isabella was the preferred Christian name, and in family circles she was known as 'Isa'. She was born in Austria. Her family, on one side, were the venerable and distinguished Venetian Giustiniani; and on the other the Bandini, who came to prominence in the Marche region of Italy. Esme Howard's own words describe some of the romantic difficulty he was facing:

> Courtship … was in Rome, even as late as 1896, no easy matter. There was no opportunity of a tête-à-tête, let alone a heart-to-heart conversation. It was not considered correct even to talk to unmarried girls for more than a quarter of an hour. 'Sitting out' at a ball was taboo. So strict indeed was the supervision in my father-in-law's house that his elder daughters … were never allowed to cross the 'anti-camera' or entrance hall of their house in Rome without a maid or a governess.[2]

Esme returned to England lovelorn and disappointed, although by now he was preoccupied by his mother's worsening health. She died soon after they got back to England and was buried at Greystoke. Esme 'recovered his balance' by staying for a few weeks at the Tower with his sister-in-law Mabel. It took Esme two more years before, in spring 1898, he could return once more to Rome. There, he plucked up the courage to write to Isabella's father, Prince Sigismondo Giustiniani Bandini, declaring his love for her and requesting an 'appointment'. He made no secret of the fact that he had little to offer Isabella apart from a happy family – no estate, little money and a career still undefined.[3] It had even occurred to him that the best he might do, should she agree to marry him, would be to look after her in a small house in the English countryside. To his surprise, the prince's reply was to offer him a date and a time. That first proper encounter with Isabella went well. Extraordinary as it may seem to modern readers, Esme on that very occasion expressed his love and she agreed to marry him. The eventual joining of two remarkable families following such a remote courtship, and with Esme's declared prospects being somewhat meagre, suggests an immediacy of true love – which was confirmed by the happy and enduring marriage that followed.

Isabella's only concern was that Esme was not a Roman Catholic and, as she put it quite bluntly, her faith was the 'first question in her life'. All Esme could profess at that time was a nominal Anglicanism. He agreed to take instruction from Monsignor Rafael Merry del Val, a family friend who was chamberlain to Pope Leo XIII and destined for high office at the Vatican. Esme confessed many of his concerns about religious faith but, step by step, the Monsignor by his side, he made his overtures to the Catholic Church, with growing conviction and a deep sense of spiritual conversion. One marvels at Esme's persistence, and we find something of that quality in Hubert, when, half a century later, he courted Lelia Caetani against a complex background not so much of social protocol but of war and uncertainty.

Esme left Rome renewed in every way, and, after a business trip to Trinidad, where he was received into the Catholic Church, he returned to Rome in October 1898 to be married. The wedding ceremony took place a month later, on 17 November, in the private chapel of the Palazzo Bandini in the Via del Sudario in Rome.[4] The day after their marriage,

Isabella Giustiniani Bandini,
the year of her marriage, 1898

and through her family's connections, Esme and Isabella went to pay their respects to Pope Leo XIII. Isabella's mother, who had been ill for some time, died on 15 December. The couple spent that Christmas at Portofino, as guests of Esme's sister Elsie, the Dowager Duchess of Carnarvon. After Portofino, and the New Year (1899), Esme and Isabella made a slow return to London, stopping off in Turin and Paris. They spent the following Christmas as guests of her father at his country home at Fiastra, in the Marche region.

In an extraordinary development, Esme now decided that the incipient civil war in South Africa was of such grave concern and that he should enlist and confront the fierce anti-British nationalism of the Boers. Motivated by idealism and his belief in the value of the Commonwealth, Esme gained Isabella's support, and, as soon as he could, enlisted as a trooper with the Middlesex Regiment (The Duke of Cambridge's Own).

In mid-February 1900, he found himself on board the rusty *Dunvegan Castle*, riding a rough sea and heading for Cape Town. The storm lasted for three days and nights. Most of the lifeboats were wrecked. The troop nevertheless made it to Cape Town on 6 March and in fine weather disembarked horses, pitched tents and prepared for the unknown. Esme was given a black cob so lazy it refused even to trot. Spring was spent at Matjiesfontein, high in the veldt of Cape Colony. Camp life grew on Esme and he made several friends. He also managed to get rid of his indolent horse.

The troop moved on to Bloemfontein, capital of the Orange Free State, where conditions rapidly deteriorated – disturbed sleep, sickness, hard work, filthy rivers in which to wash and one forced march after another. Esme wrote to Isabella at the end of May saying that they were under small arms and artillery fire. The fatalities mounted. Esme's position, by then close to the small town of Lindley, was eventually overrun in a dramatic and bloody encounter. On 31 May, Esme's entire troop was forced to surrender. He wrote that the Boers had been honourable with him and the other troopers, leaving them their money but confiscating all their letters and papers. They were, however, allowed to buy provisions in town before being marched under escort to Reitz. One evening, to their astonishment, the Boers sang 'God Save the Queen' in their honour at a camp party.

Later, after falling ill with fever, Esme was left behind at the attractive little Boer market town of Vrede in the care of an English family named Bayford. The Boers, for whom Esme developed great respect, were easy-going to the point where, after making a partial recovery, Esme and a fellow trooper managed to escape. It was 11 August and a dust storm was raging. Having climbed over the garden fence of the Bayfords' house, they hid for several hours in a cubby hole under the pulpit of a nearby Wesleyan chapel. When the hue and cry had died down, they found refuge in a house whose Boer owner had been arrested the day before for refusing to fight. After two nights, they escaped into the countryside and hid near a river, in extreme cold, until the early hours. Unable to find horses and a guide they ended up walking forty-five miles to the English camp at Volksrust. It took them three days.

The Duke of Cambridge's Own Yeomanry, Boer War, 1900
(Trooper Esme Howard at far right under 'x')

Esme Howard's gallant participation in the Boer War, which was to drag on until 1902, lasted from February to November 1900 and had been motivated by his innate sense of adventure coupled with an idealism that was perhaps rare even for those times. It is impossible not to draw a parallel between Esme's almost impulsive escapade in the cause of South Africa's freedom and Hubert's equally impulsive willingness, exactly forty years later, to join the British volunteer force that went to the aid of the beleaguered Finns.

Soon after his return to England, Esme took Isabella to Rome for Christmas and to be with her relatives. On 22 January 1901, while they were still in Rome, news came of Queen Victoria's death – an epochal event in the history of the English monarchy. In August the following year, Esme attended the coronation of King Edward VII at Westminster

Abbey, having been invited by the Duke of Norfolk (Henry Fitzalan-Howard, fifteenth duke) to be one of the many ushers or 'Gold Staff Officers'. He continued to wrestle with career issues but his heart was by now in diplomacy and, as the historian Brian McKercher puts it, Esme was 'ready to be a great diplomat'.[5] He soon accepted as a stop-gap job the role of honorary secretary at the British Embassy in Rome. Having been away from diplomacy since 1890, this seemed a good way to get back in. Indeed, he made quite a name for himself negotiating the sensitive diplomacy of King Edward's visit to Pope Leo XIII, which took place on 29 April 1903. As a result, he gained an appointment to serve as consul-general in the autonomous state of Crete, where they arrived on 11 July.

Esme and Isabella loved every aspect of Crete, and they had the joy of two periods of leave which took them back to Rome for the births of their first two sons: Esmetto on 17 October that year, and Francis on 5 October 1905. The political situation Esme faced in Crete was particularly challenging, coming so soon after the Greco-Turkish war in 1897 and the expulsion of Ottoman forces the following year. As high commissioner, Prince George of Greece and Denmark had a most difficult task. It was a period of reconstruction, and not without tension as Crete was superintended by the four great powers – Britain, France, Italy and Russia. Trying to keep the peace was a balancing act. However, Esme's natural diplomacy and almost forensic understanding of the issues involved were key to his being awarded his first appointment to the British Embassy in Washington, where they arrived in December 1906. There he served for two years as a counsellor, mainly under the highly reputed ambassador James Bryce, who served from 1907 to 1913, and of whom, as of President 'Teddy' Roosevelt, Esme became a good friend.

In terms of his work responsibilities, Esme was asked to concentrate on coordinating and improving relationships between the British dominion of Canada and the British colony of Newfoundland, and America. What was seen as a byzantine bureaucratic system in London, in which the Colonial Office had responsibility for the external affairs of Canada and Newfoundland, and the Foreign Office for relations with the United States, was as much of a hindrance as the unreliability and unfettered

Esme Howard (left) in the grounds of the White House with US Secretary of State
Charles E. Hughes and veteran French Ambassador Jean Jules Jusserand, *c.* 1924

nature of the American press. A reflection of the latter, perhaps, was that
soon after the Howards arrived in Washington the 'Functions' column of
the *New York Times*, with casual concern for the facts, referred to Isabella
as a 'charming young Englishwoman' and reported that Esme, the convert,
'being a member of the famous family of which the Duke of Norfolk is
the head, is naturally a Roman Catholic'.

Esme's successful assignment to Washington, brief though it was,
served as another stepping stone, as we shall see, to higher office. Moreover,
his pleasure in getting to know the Americans and their way of life was
enriched by the arrival of a third son, Hubert, in December 1907.

CHAPTER THREE

Ancestral Traces

I T would help any understanding of Hubert and his brothers to invoke, briefly, the history of their paternal and maternal families. In terms of the Howards, it seems appropriate to trace those historic names and epochs that particularly fascinated Hubert. To begin with, it is regrettable that the Howards should be so commonly associated with the Tudor and Elizabethan eras. Those were colourful times, admittedly, when Howards found it hard to strike an acceptable balance between distinction and disgrace. While they have been referred to as 'the noble house of Howard', Hubert's Tudor and Elizabethan ancestors are sometimes portrayed as devious and arrogant 'toffs', with a condescending attitude to the lower classes that might easily have been modelled on Aristotle's dictum that the worst kind of inequality results from trying to make unequal things equal. However, with the possible exception of Thomas (1473–1554), 3rd Duke of Norfolk, who worked tirelessly and shamelessly for his own ends, Howard history has on the whole been marked by distinction and at times by its uncomfortable adherence to Roman Catholicism. It has also been marked by highs, lows, affluence and honour imprudently lost but regained through a combination of marriage, honourable service to crown and country, considerable patience and no small degree of cunning.

Edward Fitzalan-Howard, the eighteenth and present duke, is the nation's leading Catholic layman and the Norfolk dukedom the only one to have survived intact since medieval times. Edward's ancestry can reliably be traced back to the Plantagenet King Edward I (1239–1307) who in 1254 married the Spanish Infanta, Eleanor of Castile, and in 1299 Marguerite of France. The two lines of the king's family weave this way and that, the Norfolk Howards being descended from the second marriage. Their dukedom was created for John Howard (1421–85) in recognition of gallant service to King Richard III. Both the king and he perished at the Battle of Bosworth Field (1485), which brought an end to the Wars of the Roses and ultimately to the Plantagenet dynasty. John Howard's son, Thomas (1443–1524), eventually to become the second duke, also fought at Bosworth Field but he is best remembered for his brilliant, and one must add ruthless, leadership of the English army in its defeat of the Scots at the Battle of Flodden Field, in 1513. His two sons, Thomas (later to become third duke) and Edmund, were also conspicuous at Flodden, the victory bringing much royal favour to the Howards.

In Tudor and Elizabethan times, while the Howards were strong in their service to the country, their blood ties with royalty were a recurring problem. The royal court of King Henry VIII seethed with rumour – favourites and honorary titles came and went, and it was enough for enemies of the Howards to gossip for the monarch's spies to go to work. Ever present was the axe, whose use in those times was sometimes the result of injustice, paranoia or plain cruelty. Furthermore, it could take decades for a dishonoured or attainted family to have its titles and lands restored.

So it was that the once powerful Thomas (third duke) and his son Henry Howard (c.1517–47), Earl of Surrey, were condemned to death for treason, the ailing king having been persuaded that they were plotting to usurp the monarchy. Duke Thomas, openly ambitious and necessarily political, had seen to it that two of his nieces, Anne Boleyn and Catherine Howard, became queens of England. Both young women were in due course tried and executed, respectively in 1536 and 1542, as much for the king's dynastic expedience as for their perceived disloyalty.

The fate of Thomas' son Henry, the earl (and a cousin of both the doomed queens), took many by surprise because only a year before being sent to the Tower of London, and at the age of just twenty-eight, he had been

Henry Howard, Poet Earl of Surrey, in a posthumous
portrait believed to have been commissioned by
the Collector Earl in the early 17th century

appointed the king's supreme military commander. A gifted poet in the
Petrarchan manner (he became known as the 'Poet Earl'), he was extremely
self-confident, boisterous and passionate; as a brave and colourful Howard,
few can have matched his fearless nature. His defiant and eloquent words,
at the trial and on the scaffold, were, however, not enough to save him.[1]
The earl was executed on 19 January 1547, and his father would have
followed him a week later had King Henry VIII himself not died on the
eve of his execution.

Thomas Howard (1536–72), 4th Duke of Norfolk, son of the tragic
earl, was astute enough to marry his three sons to the daughters of
his third wife, Anne Dacre, thereby gaining practically the whole of
Cumberland for the Howards. In other ways Thomas lacked judgment
and unfortunately was to suffer a similar fate to that of his father, this

time under Queen Elizabeth I. Once again, the accusation was that of plotting against the monarch. The duke, it is true, had considered plans to marry Mary, Queen of Scots, and so to restore England to the Catholic faith. His confessional pleadings to Elizabeth, to whom he was related, were not enough to save his life. He was put to death in 1572, yet another tragic figure in Howard history. After his death, Mary, who would herself be executed by Elizabeth in 1587, observed: 'Alas, what has the House of Howard suffered for my sake.'[2] After Thomas' death, the dukedom went into abeyance for eighty-eight years.

Of all Hubert's direct ancestors, the one whom he most admired was the fourth duke's eldest son, the martyr St Philip Howard (1557–95), whose short life epitomised the family's oscillations between triumph and tragedy. He was named Philip after his godfather King Philip II of Spain. He captures the imagination because of the contradictions in his life: his Protestant upbringing (even though he was baptised a Catholic), his arranged marriage to Anne Dacre, his move to court when he was eighteen, his virtual abandonment of his wife, his amorous adventures and the eventual recovery of his moral compass. His return to the Roman Catholic Church, in 1584, owed much to the influence of the martyr Edmund Campion and to that of his saintly and forgiving wife. Warned of danger, Philip attempted with other members of his family to move to France to practise his faith freely. As a second cousin to the queen, his action was deemed still more of a betrayal; however, his letter asking for her permission to move abroad had been intercepted and never delivered. Thrown into the Tower of London in 1585, he was further accused of praying for the success of the Spanish Armada which attacked England in 1588. While no charges of high treason were ever proved, he was held under sentence of death for a decade, loved by many of his enemies and refusing to abandon his faith even though it meant losing everything. He died of dysentery at the Tower, aged thirty-eight.

Philip was at the leading edge of the Counter-Reformation and the heroic years of recusancy, when many adherents of the old religion went 'underground' for fear of the Protestant inquisition. Arundel Cathedral, standing close to the Howards' historic seat of Arundel Castle, now bears his name, and there is a chapel there to honour him. He is also featured in a modern statue, complete with faithful dog – better sculpted than the master. It is hard to be unmoved by Philip's stoicism, a curiously morbid Tudor disposition, and his understanding of the value of accepting suffering on this earth, not for its own sake but for the sake of Christ. Above the fireplace of his cell in the Tower of London, Philip carved an inscription in Latin that translates as: 'The more afflictions we endure for Christ in this world, the more glory we shall attain with Christ in the next.' Philip was beatified in 1929, and in 1970 raised to the altars as one of the Forty English Martyrs canonised by Pope Paul VI.

St Philip's only son, Thomas (1585–1646), 14th Earl of Arundel, is notable for entirely different reasons. Known later as the 'Collector Earl', he emerged penniless from the family setbacks to become one of the greatest of the early English private collectors. His lavish expenditure on art and the cultivation of artist friends throughout Europe was another effort, no doubt, to restore prestige to the Howard family. Rubens, whose career he helped foster, referred to him as the 'evangelist of art'. In all his work as a collector and patron, he was much helped by the immense inheritances of his wife, Alethea Talbot, whom he married in 1606. At its height, Thomas' collection amounted to 700 paintings, while his marbles, gems, prints and drawings were unrivalled at the time.

The present Duke of Norfolk has worked hard to revitalise the Arundel estates and is a welcoming steward of the castle, today one of the finest tourist attractions in the south of England. The building itself stands high above the river Arun, in West Sussex, which snakes lazily through luxuriant meadows in the valley below and lends its waters to an array of ponds that make up the thirty-five-acre Arundel Wetlands Centre. The castle's oldest feature is an eleventh-century motte or mound, which dominates the courtyard. The castle's association with the Norfolk dukes goes back 850 years. Just as Cromwell's armies damaged Greystoke Castle during the English Civil War, that lasted from 1642 to 1651, so they damaged Arundel. Centuries of repairs were carried out, some by Charles, the eleventh duke; the most recent by Henry, fifteenth duke, who was among the first in this country to install electricity in a private

Arundel Castle from the river Arun

building. Regularly in demand as a film set, the castle is a magical and otherworldly place. Its art collection includes works by Van Dyck, Rubens, Gainsborough, Reynolds, Canaletto and Millais. The portrait gallery hosts a fine chronological display of all the Norfolk dukes. There is a splendid library, a baronial hall, an armoury, various chapels and superb gardens.

GIUSTINIANI HISTORY is no less replete with colour and distinction, twists and turns. The family's origins are Venetian, but the Giustiniani settled centuries ago in Genoa and were to be found also in Naples, Corsica and the Greek islands (curiously, members of the Genoese branch of the Giustiniani were, until 1566, the owners and rulers of Chios, the fifth largest of those islands). The Marquess Vincenzo Giustiniani (1564–1637), whose father was the last ruler of Chios, emerged as a noted art collector who moved to Rome and became a patron of Caravaggio. There, at the Palazzo Giustiniani, he is known to have entertained Thomas Howard, the Collector Earl.

The Venetian Giustiniani had particularly close links to the papacy. Notable among them was the saint and patriarch of Venice, Lorenzo Giustiniani (1381–1456), and the doge Marcantonio Giustiniani (1619–88). To their distinguished number may be added several senators, high-ranking members of religious orders, and brave soldiers who brought honour to the family name.

The Venetian Giustiniani are no longer, and they came close to dying out eight centuries ago in circumstances that linger today in the minds and records of some descendants and can be traced back to the wars of the twelfth century, when the Venetian Republic was struggling to maintain its maritime supremacy in the region.[3] All the male members of the Giustiniani family except Nicolò Giustiniani, a monk at San Nicolò del Lido, had been killed during Doge Vitale II Michiel's disastrous war against the then Byzantine emperor, Manuel I Comneno, and by a severe plague which coincided with the doge's last ill-fated naval action against the Byzantines in 1152.

The Venetians, distressed at the potential extinction of one of their great families, sent a public petition to Pope Alexander III, who permitted Nicolò to be laicised and to marry Anna, a daughter of the doge. The brutal murder of Vitale II Michiel a few months later, at the hands of a mob seeking vengeance for his failures, was to some extent mitigated by the fact that this unlikely couple produced nine boys and three girls. His duty accomplished, and when the youngest son was twelve, Nicolò returned to his monastery; Anna took vows and entered the convent of Sant'Ariano di Costanziaco, which she is said to have founded. Hubert, being an historian and a Catholic, was doubtless aware that, in theory at least, he was descended from a monk and a nun.[4]

THE BANDINI family, of which there were a number of branches, were known as far back as the twelfth century in the town of Camerino, in the Italian province of Macerata. They gained distinction through public service and patronage of the arts. By degrees, from the eighteenth century, they developed close ties with the papacy. The double family name Giustiniani Bandini no longer exists, but is worth explanation. It derived from the marriage, in 1815, of Cecilia Giustiniani, Duchess of Mondragone (and Countess of Newburgh), and Carlo Bandini, Marquess of Lanciano and Rustano.[5] Their eldest son, Sigismondo, married Maria Sofia Massani in 1848 and was created the first Prince Giustiniani Bandini by Pope Pius IX in 1863.

Sigismondo and Maria Sofia had ten children, one of whom, Isabella, was Hubert's mother. Of her siblings, the eldest, Nicoletta, died when she was five, and the fourth and tenth, respectively Carlo (who would have inherited) and Anna Maria, died in infancy. Isabella and her remaining siblings lived to great ages, none more so than Elena, who outlived her husband, Camillo Rospigliosi, by forty-five years. Hubert knew his Italian aunts well, in particular Carolina, who often had the Howard brothers to stay when they were young, and Maria Cristina and Maria Cecilia, both of whom were charmingly eccentric.

Zia (Aunt) Maria Cristina, known as 'Kri' and sometimes 'Kri Kri', was more or less bedridden and very blind in the last years of her life. As a young woman she had had to abandon her vocation as a Dominican nun due to ill health; however, her life was one of extraordinary dedication to charitable and religious causes. She had been instrumental, for example, in the formation of the emancipatory Union of Catholic Women in Italy. At a 1908 audience with her old friend Pius X, she offered to become its head. The pope demurred and quoted from an old Venetian dictum to the effect that a woman should be 'sweet, silent and stay at home'.[6] In 1909, Pius changed his position and Maria Cristina became the Union's first head. It grew in only a few years to a membership of 30,000. Maria Cristina was an unforgettable character. One Christmas, a friend gave her a live chicken that, instead of meeting its Yuletide destiny, roamed freely throughout her apartment, roosting by night on the metal headboard of her bed. She died in 1959.

Zia Maria Cecilia, known as 'Bebetta', whose frailty and magnificent Bandini nose gave her an air of supreme nobility, was born in 1871. As the Bandini were so close to the papacy and were members of the so-called 'black nobility', she felt keenly the aftermath of the dissolution of the Papal States in 1870, the humiliation of Pius IX, the notion of Italy as a republic and the demise of Italy's monarchy in 1946.[7] In 1920, she married the aristocratic general, Count Paolo Piella, who died in 1952. One imagined they had separated, as she never wore black or spoke about him. She had a wide circle of friends and whenever she left her apartment in Via Salaria to visit them, often for the day, she invariably draped a royalist flag over her balcony.

Another formidable Giustiniani Bandini lady, a cousin who was particularly close to Hubert, was Maria Sofia, Countess Gravina. She lived at the elegant Casa Bandini in Rome and at the spectacular early-Renaissance family castle Rocca di Lanciano, in the Marche, given to her as a wedding present. Her father, a brother of Donna Isabella's, was named Carlo after his deceased sibling and on the death of Sigismondo in 1908 became the second Prince Giustiniani Bandini as well as the ninth Earl of Newburgh.[8] Her mother, Maria Lanza di Trabia, came from a grand old Sicilian family.

In 1922, Maria Sofia married the diplomat, Count Manfredi Gravina di Ramacca, who died ten years later. Thereafter she remained in perpetual mourning for him, dressed in black like other widows in high Roman society. She had two brothers, Sigismondo and Giuseppe, the latter known as 'Joey'. They both died before their father, upon whose death, in 1941, Maria Sofia became the tenth Countess of Newburgh. Distinguished and gentle, she spoke four languages fluently and had a touching, almost feudal, rapport with her community of farmers in the Marche, whose children she educated. Devoted to charitable causes, she became chair in the 1960s of what is now the Figlie della Carità (The Daughters of Charity), an offshoot of the Society of St Vincent de Paul.

In 1974, she set up the Giustiniani Bandini Foundation, as willed by her brother Sigismondo, who had died in 1918. Into this she transferred the magnificent family palazzo, the Palazzo dei Principi, which they had acquired from the papal government in about 1773, and the adjacent historic Cistercian abbey of Fiastra, to which monks returned in 1985 only to depart again in 2018. The abbey estate, of some 4,500 acres, is now

Princess Maria Sofia Giustiniani Bandini (married name
Gravina), one of Hubert's closest first cousins

a government-recognised nature reserve. In all, the family estates once
extended to five communes in the Province of Macerata.

Maria Sofia died in 1977. In her will, she left Rocca di Lanciano to
the bishopric of Camerino, and almost everything else to the Vatican.
Hubert, as her executor, was landed with the unenviable task of handling
the complex arrangements. Since Maria Sofia had no heirs, the Newburgh
title passed to Prince Giulio Cesare Rospigliosi, her first cousin once
removed, and thence to his son Filippo, the twelfth earl, born in 1942.
Three great and interrelated historic families – Giustiniani, Bandini and
Rospigliosi – together made up one of Italy's richest blends of Roman
Catholic earldoms and principalities, producing a bewildering array of
titles, some of which it must be said have little more than honorific or
even nostalgic value in the modern, secular Republic of Italy.

CHAPTER FOUR

Between the Wars

A FTER service in Washington, which concluded in 1908, Esme
Howard was posted successively to Budapest, where his fourth
son Mondi was born, and Berne. These postings were challenging, but during his time in neutral Switzerland Esme had developed a deep
and almost prophetic personal suspicion of Germany. His next period
of service was in Stockholm, from 1913 to 1918. The eruption of World
War I in 1914 may not have been a complete surprise, but as envoy at the
British Legation it was his job to discern Swedish intentions in the light
of the country's pro-German and Russo-phobic leanings. Trapped now
by the proximity of Germany's warmongering, much as he had foreseen it,
Esme's task was particularly challenging. Had he not been instrumental in
keeping the Swedes from entering the war on the side of Germany, things
might have turned out very differently.[1]

While home tuition at the legation was effective up to a point, Esmetto
and Francis became increasingly impatient with their governess and so, in
1917, and at considerable risk since the war was not yet at an end, their
father sent them on an admiralty passenger ship across the heavily mined
North Sea, to attend Downside boarding school in Somerset, England.
At no stage was the ship escorted, and it navigated a route from Bergen
to Aberdeen via the Shetlands, zigzagging and keeping all its lights turned
off. In old age, Francis remembered that voyage as having been one of
the most frightening experiences of his life. Even before the war ended

Isabella Howard with Mondi (left) and Hubert, *c.* 1912

Left to right: Francis, Mondi, Hubert
and Esmetto in Berne, *c.* 1913

Left to right: Hubert, Henry and
Mondi, Stockholm, *c.* 1915

officially in November 1918, the rest of the family returned to England. Hubert joined Esmetto and Francis at Downside in September, aged ten. He would remain there for six years. Mondi followed in 1920, while Henry joined the school in 1922.

Several generations of Howards were to attend Downside, run by the Benedictines. South of the old Roman city of Bath, the site is dominated by a fine neo-Gothic abbey church, completed in 1925, soon after the first batch of Howard brothers had left. Boarding-school life was austere in those times, the disciplines harsh, the religious observances frequent. The echoing dormitories and classrooms were cold and bleak, fed by endless corridors. For the boys, the black jackets, striped trousers and stiff collars added to the sense of being forcibly institutionalised. Esmetto survived well enough, even though he suffered from poor health and general frailty. Francis so utterly disliked his time there that he eventually sent his sons to Ampleforth, another Benedictine school, in the north of England.

Hubert coped well at Downside, although, like his brothers, he deplored the snobbishness of its then headmaster. In his first term he came out top in History, which set him on the path towards that academic specialism. From afar, Hubert's 'Mammina' fretted about his daily ration of cod liver oil, and he dutifully replied to her letters. If doing so in Italian, which he often did, he addressed her as 'tu'; if in French, 'vous'. It is noticeable the extent to which Hubert's writing improved after he joined the school. Around the age of seven, Hubert had written an undated letter to his mother and to Mondi. He had been invited away from Stockholm to stay with English friends of his parents in Kalmar County. Perhaps due to his conversing so often in his mother's native Italian, and being otherwise subject to nursery tuition at the British Legation residence, his written English was clearly in need of improvement.

The following extract is an example of his charmingly childish spelling: 'and at the stashon we bort some Straberies. It is very nice hear, there are Cheritrees and Straberes, Rasberies, Graps, Gousberes, and I have ridden a horse called Cleopatra'. It is extraordinary, in the circumstances, that he managed to spell Cleopatra correctly.

At Downside Hubert began to mature, although soon after his arrival
at the school, and as the war ended, he exclaimed patriotically in a letter to
his parents that 'the Germans have been absolutely squashed'. (Downside
had lost many of its pupils to the war and yet the boys continued for
decades thereafter to play out, in the inter-school *mêlées* that took place
each weekend on the rugby fields, the old dreams of imperial triumph.)

Many years later, in a letter to Francis dated 3 March 1924, when he
was sixteen and Francis had already left the school, Hubert gave vent
to his still adolescent views on music, and in so doing (perhaps because
his opinions were passionately held), displayed vestiges of his childhood
tendency to scramble his grammar and spelling:

> I write to you in Red Ink, because I want to economise my blue ink.
> Your letter was very funny, but for shame, what are your tastes in music
> coming to. I do not mind you liking beautiful pieces composed by great
> modern writers but after all Beethoven is perfectly wonderful. Have
> you heard his 3rd, 5th and 7th symphonies? [...] Hear them as soon
> as you can and then appreciate Beethoven. About Hoffman I know
> little ... I like Bach at times but you must admit that a great number
> (the <u>greater</u> number!!) of his things are very dull. As for Wagner (the
> greatest orchestral composer) some of his things are so dull that they
> nearly send me to sleep. Take for example Tristan and Isolda. The
> first Act – unbearable, second Act – unbearable for the greater part
> (King Marc – Oh!!) but is it not worth while to be tortured for about
> three hours in order to hear the end? Of course it is!, for the end is the
> greatest masterpiece in music ever written.

Esme and Isabella corresponded for the most part in Italian, and, when
she wrote to him, he was her 'maritello carissimo' ('dearest little husband').
He and she gained much pleasure from the fact that Hubert enjoyed his
Catholic school, and the spiritual dimension of life in close proximity to
a monastic community. The young Hubert, whatever the evolution of
his grammar, certainly loved music and liturgy, revelling in Gregorian
plainchant and the great solemnity of the High Masses celebrated each

Sunday. All this led Hubert to a moving affirmation of his faith, probably coinciding with his confirmation, which he described in his diary as a 'profound sentiment of religion, essentially intuitive, that requires no thinking or reason but is a state of truth; it pours itself out in love'. During those Downside years he was influenced by Thomas à Kempis, the fifteenth-century Dutch-German canon, whose *The Imitation of Christ* is among the best-selling devotional books ever written.[2]

Mondi's experience of Downside was less favourable, and he persuaded his father, as soon as the latter took up his appointment as British Ambassador to Washington in 1924, to move him out to America. There, for a while, he attended the Newman Catholic School in Lakewood, New Jersey. In contrast, their younger brother Henry appeared to get on well at Downside, but was indignant that his parents had decided to move to Washington. With some thought to completing his schooling in America, he accompanied his parents to Washington in summer 1924. Eventually, his father sent Henry back to Downside to gain more discipline.

WHILE THE boys were at Downside, and before his final diplomatic appointment to Washington, Esme Howard served as ambassador to Madrid, from 1919 to 1924. The boys went out there as often as it was affordable, to stay with their parents at the embassy residence at 16 Calle de Fernando El Santo. On their first visit, over Christmas 1919, their father, now Sir Esme, read them Cervantes' *Don Quixote*, from cover to cover. Within a short time, the boys began to manifest their genetic 'Howard stubbornness' and capacity for sibling rivalries – a sure sign of mutual affection. Indeed, Hubert's love of orderliness was never below the surface. On a later holiday at the Madrid residence, he drew an imaginary line in a clothes drawer that he shared with Mondi. When, inevitably, one of Mondi's undergarments strayed across the invisible frontier, Hubert flung it out of the window where it lodged for days on a tram wire.

During the period of Esme Howard's ambassadorship in Madrid, the political scene was a considerable challenge to him. Indeed, in his first dispatch to the Foreign Office in January 1920, he reported that the country was on the verge of a 'very dangerous crisis' due to labour unrest, the political ambitions of the military junta and the instability of the government itself. Tension between the government and the military escalated to the point when, on 13 September 1922, a coup d'état did take place, the machinations of which were explained to Esme by King Alfonso XIII, and relayed personally by him, at the king's request, to the English monarch George V. By the time Esme and Isabella left Spain, General Primo de Rivera, who did not fit Esme's idea of a dictator, was the most powerful man in the country and indeed perceived by Esme as having 'statesmanlike qualities'.[3]

A charming story accompanies Esme's appointment to Washington in 1924. When Lord Curzon, the Foreign Secretary at that time, offered him the prestigious post, Esme did not consider himself 'conspicuous' enough for the job. He penned a letter to Curzon in which, struggling for an excuse, he pleaded that Isabella was apt to be hopelessly sick at sea. The letter was handed to a Spanish diplomat friend who was, however, unexpectedly waylaid in Paris on his journey back to London. By the time Curzon received the letter, he had already secured the king's assent. There was no turning back.

The extraordinary complexities of Anglo-American relations at the time of Esme taking up his new appointment were driven mostly by Britain's indebtedness to America and by its enviable naval power. Such strains, and others, were in turn exacerbated by internal divisions and competing perspectives on both sides. Rapprochement was the declared diplomatic goal but suspicion was inflamed by the press on both sides of the Atlantic. It was central to Esme's ambassadorial and personal perspective, and to the goals of Alanson B. Houghton, his American counterpart in London, who served as American Ambassador from 1925 to 1929, that peace be kept. With his earlier imperial sympathies but also his strong sense of the need for union between English-speaking nations, Esme was equally keen to strengthen Britain's worldwide prestige. He went widely on tour in America, lecturing and building bridges with businessmen and industrialists. He exhausted himself in the process and was particularly demotivated by the brouhaha surrounding the inconclusive 1927 Geneva Naval Disarmament Conference, between Britain, America and Japan – with its sombre implications for arms limitation, trade blockades, maritime law and the freedom of the seas. As extraordinary as it may now seem, there was fierce speculation as to the possibility of a military confrontation between Britain and America.

The Howard brothers were impressed by the novelty of Washington and other American cities. They occasionally went up to New York to see the sights and imbibe the culture. One of Hubert's lifelong friends was the writer Iris Origo, née Cutting, who, soon after her marriage in 1924 to Marchese Antonio Origo, went to visit her widowed grandmother Olivia Cutting in New York City. She recalled how, while staying there, Hubert and one of his brothers were not only invited to the Cutting house, but also treated to several performances at the Metropolitan Opera, where the family had a box. The origins of this connection were almost certainly diplomatic in that Olivia's son, Iris' father William Bayard Cutting Jr, had served as secretary to the American Ambassador to London.[4]

The first three years of Esme Howard's ambassadorship in Washington, from 1924 to 1926, were cruelly overshadowed for the entire family by the declining health and eventual death of Esmetto. Having taken his degree at Oxford's New College in summer 1924, which he did in spite of great and unexplained physical suffering throughout his examination year, Esmetto then joined his parents in America for a holiday in Beverley, near Boston, where the doctors diagnosed Hodgkin's Lymphoma, seldom curable in those days. The holiday over, Esmetto travelled with his mother to a hotel in Mürren, in the Bernese Alps, where it was hoped that the mountain air would alleviate his discomfort. The last time the entire family would be together was in summer 1925. The sadness was palpable and they would sit in silence, lost for words. Every effort was made to find a cure but no remission came. In early 1926, Esmetto was moved to the Rocher Clinic in Berne, where, in spite of his frailty, he managed a letter to his parents following a visit from Hubert, in which with characteristic humour he wrote of his brother: 'A spot of ink on a tablecloth still gives him a lot of worry.' In September, as the

At the Swiss clinic, 1925, the last gathering of all the family before Esmetto's death.
From left to right: Mondi, Esmetto, Hubert, Isabella, Francis, Henry and Esme

situation worsened, Esmetto's parents moved him to Guy's Hospital in London, where some new treatment offered a faint ray of hope. Tragically, however, Esmetto contracted pneumonia and died at a nursing home in Hampstead on 15 November 1926.

ALTHOUGH HE HAD disliked Downside, Francis did well academically, gaining a place at Trinity College, Cambridge, in 1923. In this august institution, founded by Henry VIII in 1546, he took a degree in law, gaining a scholarship to Harvard Law School before joining J. P. Morgan in 1927. In 1925, as his eldest brother's health began seriously to deteriorate, Hubert followed Francis to Trinity College, to read History. On the surface, Hubert was an exemplary student, cultivating a wide circle of international friends and taking his studies seriously. Weather permitting, he enjoyed regular games of hockey, and when it rained he played squash or other indoor games. The loss of his brother in autumn 1926, however, utterly demoralised him. He went into a period of mourning; his letters throughout 1927 were bordered in black. The grief may account for some of his soul-searching and mood fluctuations while at university. His last year at Cambridge was one of 'greatest happiness and greatest sorrow... I was stretched between Heaven and Hell almost to breaking point ... I moved in kingdoms wider than our own. Yet never did I feel more miserable, more imprisoned'. A further manifestation of his mood was a lack of confidence in his ability to pass his final exams at Cambridge. He would declare this in letters to his father, as if to prepare him for the worst.

In the event Hubert graduated successfully in summer 1928 – just one year before the devastating Wall Street Crash. Wanting to perfect

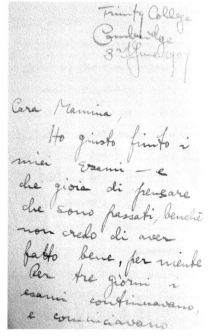

From Hubert's May 1925 letter to his parents about Henry going to Washington

From Hubert's June 1927 letter to his mother from Cambridge, after Part I of his exams, expressing doubts as to the results

Left to right: Hubert, Francis and Mondi, British Embassy, Washington, *c.* 1928

his German, he moved in early autumn to Salzburg, Austria. There, when the snow arrived, he took up cross-country skiing, a sport close to his childhood experience of walking the hills and valleys of his beloved Cumberland. In November, before this had transpired, Hubert wrote a note to his mother in Italian, telling her that he had lost weight, which he attributed (clearly improbably) to his lack of exercise, and lamenting his lack of progress with German: 'Se un potere santo non mi aiuta [*sic*], non vedo come a [*sic*] superare questa lingua barbara, che, come le teste e le code d'un dragone, e imbrogliato in una confusione senza ragionamento.' ('Unless a heavenly power should come to my aid, I do not see how I am going to master this barbaric language which, like the heads and tails of a dragon, is entangled in an irrational confusion.')

In French, again from Salzburg, he wrote another letter to his mother, who was on her way back to England from Washington, ahead of her husband. His choice of travel-ware and creature comforts displays his already discriminating tastes:

> Est-ce-que vous auriez le temps à Londres de m'acheter plusieurs choses dont j'ai besoin? ... Il me faut absolument un nouveau petit coffre – la marque s'appelle 'Revelation suitcases', et je crois qu'ils ne coûtent pas plus de 18 schellings. Puis, j'aimerais du Yardley Lavender shaving soap et du Coal Tar soap.

> Might you have time in London to buy me a number of things I need? ... I absolutely require a new small suitcase – the brand name is 'Revelation suitcases' [these expandable suitcases had become all the rage] and I do not think it would cost more than 18 shillings. I would also love some Yardley Lavender shaving soap and some Coal Tar soap as well.

In December, still based in Salzburg, Hubert made a three-week tour of Germany, taking in Munich, Nuremberg, Bamberg, Berlin and Dresden.

In spite of all his activities and distractions, Hubert's Salzburg diary reveals him to have plunged again into a period of religious introspection, loneliness and existential malaise.[5] Its pages are filled with quotations from poets, philosophers and historians. His love of art, beauty and truth appears everywhere in his writings, and beyond that is his recurring sense of his own mortality and how peace is only achievable by following the will of God. In one entry, he quotes the famous last line of François de Malherbe's poem of consolation to his friend M. du Périer, who had lost his daughter: 'Vouloir ce que Dieu veut est la seule science qui nous met en repos' ('To want what God wills is the only way to find peace').

During this period Hubert committed to a daily programme, beginning at 6 a.m. with 'morning prayers, followed by a period of physical exercise, a walk or a run followed by a cold bath, Mass, breakfast and dealing with the day's mail'. All this was to be accomplished before resuming his studies at 10 a.m. Recreation was from 6 to 8 p.m. followed by dinner, a period for reading, and bed at 10.30 p.m. Hubert also filled his Salzburg diary with birthday lists of his close relations and godchildren, to help him with

Hubert Howard, *c.* 1931

the many gifts he made to them in his lifetime; nor did he overlook the names of those departed whom he wished to remember in his prayers. In February 1930, as his father steamed back to England on the liner *Majestic* following his retirement from Washington and the diplomatic life, Hubert wrote to congratulate him for his 'brilliant and long career' while lamenting that his depressions would see him 'at the bottom of the list of academic failures'.

This period of heightened emotions, of self-imposed discipline and austerity, and of that sense of loneliness which surfaces repeatedly in his writings, seemed to reach an apogee at Easter 1929, when he went briefly to Paris to study French, lodging in the Rue Madame. From there he wrote several letters to Francis, one of which expressed his frustration at having been forced out of cheap lodgings in the Rue Vavin, above a nightclub, where from midnight to four in the morning 'all that is most loathsome in this world (wealth, cathode tube electric light, intoxication, servility, noise) runs riot'. He soon returned to the theme of his solitude, which he felt was tolerable when he was in close proximity to friends and family, but hard to bear without them: 'What allows me to exist, to vegetate, is that I have learnt to work…I no longer move free by myself, to radiate out as I did (with a feeble yet warm glow) at Cambridge.'

Hubert's subsequent musings are evidence of his preoccupation with the darkness in the world – 'lust, egotism, pride and covetousness' – and his longing for the transcendent. Drawing on his keen knowledge of art and philosophy, he expresses regret at how, in so many traditions, the sensual contaminates the transcendent, although this mixture 'produces the greatest that we have – a Thomas Aquinas, a Matthias Grünewald, a Hans Holbein, a Thomas More, a John Milton, a Johann Sebastian Bach'.[6] Hubert's personal turmoil, a combination of intense religiosity and a burgeoning thirst for knowledge, never really died out during his days as a bachelor, but he had now to face up to the greater challenge of finding himself a career.

HUBERT'S FIRST instinct, unsurprisingly, was to become a diplomat. Although he had passed a Foreign Office entrance qualification before his time in Salzburg, there were few jobs available. In 1932, he made several forays into business, eventually transferring to New York to open an office for the Sheed and Ward publishing group and to begin expanding its operations into South America. Sheed and Ward had been founded in London in 1926 with a specifically Catholic identity, publishing some of the major figures of the twentieth-century Catholic literary hierarchy: G. K. Chesterton, Hilaire Belloc, Christopher Dawson and Ronald Knox. (Knox would later preside over Hubert's marriage, in 1951, to Lelia Caetani.) Hubert was in charge of the firm's offices on fashionable Fifth Avenue, and very much enjoyed the work: 'I could hardly be more satisfied,' he wrote to Mondi in February 1934. Business was good, even so soon after the Wall Street Crash.

Mondi (left) and Francis rowing together, *c.* 1933

From New York, Hubert wrote quite frequently to his family. It appears from this correspondence that, although well settled at work, he was constantly preoccupied by the issue of social justice. He wrote, for example, about how in November 1933 he had been with a friend to see a new settlement on the Upper East Side of the city on 70th Street, a run-down quarter then but highly fashionable today. The experience had left him deeply moved, because there he had witnessed a hub of valuable social and educational activities, from children's groups to operatic societies (the latter involving many Italians from the local community), and from pottery and other art forms to sports – all of these 'bringing peace, happiness and justice to a great number of people'.

His friend, a Miss Manning, social worker and founder of the settlement, persuaded him to become editor-in-chief of a newspaper that would record its activities. Following a tender for a suitable name, the paper emerged in February 1934 as the *Yorkville Advance*. Under Hubert's editorial supervision, it got off to a good start, but, within two months, Hubert and his team were affronted by the volte-face of a wealthy sponsor who, having incorporated the paper as part of his publishing company, Lennox Hill Press Inc., to protect it from libel, insisted that it be managed for profit. This went against Hubert's instincts. The immediate crisis must somehow have passed, however, as Hubert remained in charge of the paper throughout that summer.

A further example of Hubert's commitment to social justice was his growing fascination with Dorothy Day (1877–1949) and the Catholic Worker Movement, which she founded in New York in 1933. Its newspaper, the *Catholic Worker*, was designed to articulate the Movement's outreach to 'those who worked with hand or brain, those who did physical, mental, or spiritual work and those who were poor, dispossessed or exploited'.[7] Communism had become a popular ideology in America during the Depression, but the *Catholic Worker* was in no sense an ideological tool, rather it was a means of spreading the Church's radical teachings on social justice. It is interesting, here, to note Hubert's contemporaneous leaning towards the new Democrat government of Franklin D. Roosevelt and his proposals for tackling the national debt, and creating a 'New Deal' for the more deprived classes of American society.[8]

Hubert's love of the wild, and of adventure, contrasts so often in his writings and actions with his existential musings and recurring sense of loneliness. In summer 1934, he sailed back to England, paid a visit to Lyulph's Tower, and joined his brothers for a walking and climbing holiday in the Julian Alps. At New Year 1935, he went on a Canadian skiing holiday with a large party of friends; two months later he had once more 'enclosed' himself on a retreat, this time at the Jesuit Centre in Wernersville, Pennsylvania, from where he wrote that 'it is in such a place that the greatest proof for the existence of God exists'.

Back in New York, Hubert began to develop in his mind the idea of entering politics, imagining a British centrist party built explicitly according to Catholic principles. He wrote to Mondi about this on 19 February 1935:

It would prevent one from giving one's allegiance to the miserable status quo of conservatism or to the pure materialism and sexualism and irresponsibility of a fumbling socialism … I would devote my life to it, giving up all prospect of wealth, comfort, marriage or anything else.

This particular flight of altruistic fantasy did not last long, for Hubert, already alert to the emerging threat to peace posed by the fascist regimes of Germany and Italy – by this time the Second Italo-Ethiopian War was already raging – wrote again to Mondi on 22 September: 'If war comes, I suppose I shall be back with you, having as consolation the thought that I shall love our enemy,' and placing emphasis on the 'inconsequence of life or death'. In his reference to 'our enemy', was Hubert referring to his love of the German-speaking people? Or to a sense that Italy would enter the war on the side of the Germans? Or simply to the Christian injunction to love one's enemies?

In what was perhaps his last letter to Mondi from America, dated 1 December 1935, Hubert expresses his profound joy at hearing that Mondi was engaged. He wrote, 'For what a great and incomprehensible and infinitely beautiful thing Love is … in it I see the fulfilment of the Divine Will … it is the highest decision a man can take, who is not called to the priesthood.' In 1936, Hubert secured an excellent London-based job with the Carnegie Endowment's Institute for International Affairs, and moved back to London. In summer 1937 he took a long break from work to help some American friends sail a large yacht around the Aegean Islands.

MONDI AND HENRY, the two younger brothers, took different paths from one another after their school days were over. Mondi followed his late brother Esmetto to New College to study law, after which, and against Hubert's advice, he went on to practise as a barrister without very much success. Henry, in contrast, joined the Royal Military Academy at Sandhurst where, in 1933, he gained the coveted Sword of Honour, awarded to the outstanding cadet. In search of adventure, like his father and brothers, Henry joined the Somali Camel Corps, before returning to London in 1937 and joining the Council of European Bondholders. He then volunteered for a BBC initiative to broadcast to Italy – a brief opportunity for him to make use of his Italian. In 1938, and with a second world war growing ever closer, he was recalled to the Coldstream Guards in the rank of captain.

Both Mondi and Henry married well before Francis and Hubert: Mondi, in 1936, to Cécile Geoffroy-Dechaume, who came from an extensive French family of notable artists, musicians and patriots; and Henry, in 1937, to Adèle Le Bourgeois Alsop, whose family was American. Her mother, Julia, née Chapin, was a first cousin of Marguerite Chapin, who in 1911 married Roffredo Caetani, Prince of Bassiano, and who eventually became Hubert's mother-in-law.[9]

HUBERT'S FATHER Esme, having retired from Washington in 1930, and in recognition of his distinguished career, was raised to the peerage to become Baron Howard of Penrith, the town of Penrith being the closest to Greystoke Castle where he had been born. In various tributes he was described as 'one of the most gifted and important British diplomats in the first third of the twentieth century'.[10]

The last phase of Esme and Isabella's life together was spent for the most part in Surrey, where Esme took a course in bookbinding. In the autumn of 1930, he took Francis on a valedictory visit to the West Indies, where he described the Leeward and Westward Islands as 'a most glorious chaplet of pearls of great price'. In early spring 1931, he embarked with Isabella on a tour of the Holy Land. In spite of the distracting undercurrents of religious division, particularly in Jerusalem, the experience of retracing Christ's steps affected them both deeply. They returned to England in stages, stopping first in Rome to meet relatives and then meeting up with their sons in Siena at the start of the Easter holidays.

In Rome, the British Ambassador, Ronald Graham, suggested Esme might like to meet Benito Mussolini. Esme agreed as a matter of courtesy, but with severe inner reservations. At the appointed hour he was shown into the dictator's vast office, the Sala del Mappamondo in Palazzo Venezia, which his subordinates were made to cross at the double to avoid wasting his time. Esme walked in alone, not knowing what to expect. Without looking up, Mussolini pointed to where Esme was to sit, keeping him waiting until he had finished what he was doing. After an awkward start to the conversation, Mussolini asked Esme if he knew anything about Italy and whether he had observed any developments since the war. Esme replied by saying he was married to an Italian, had lived and worked there for quite some years and was pleased in particular by the resurgence of agriculture in the country. Mussolini sprang to his feet and, after denouncing the adverse impact of industrialisation on British agriculture, came up with a passionate but bombastic declaration of his own intentions, which Esme paraphrases in his autobiography as follows:

> I am building market towns in the Pontine Marshes, and in the Maremma, which will be surrounded by peasants cultivating their own lands, the aim being that every farm or holding should be sufficiently near for the children to get easily to school and the housewife to market, and the men to go in for relaxation after their day's work and see films and learn what is going on in the world and hear good music on the radios. Each of these market towns must have its church, its school and its hospital, its public library and its theatre.

In the course of this arrogant and self-serving peroration, Mussolini spoke of how he was draining the Pontine Marshes, an area which Esme said he knew well from his excursions there as a junior member of the Rome embassy in the mid-1880s. Most Italians were already seduced by fascist pragmatism. Indeed, in this period of 'Mussomania', Pius XI declared enthusiastically that Mussolini had been sent by God. However, there was an inevitable twist in regard to the marshes. Once they were finally drained, by means of Gelasio Caetani's engineering techniques and armies of immigrant labour provided by the Italian state, Mussolini confiscated almost all the Caetani property within the land reclamation area, developed new towns such as Littoria (now Latina) and Sabaudia, appointed fascist mayors and had himself photographed stripped to the waist, posing as a man of the soil and a friend of the common man. It is not hard to understand why Esme, who disagreed profoundly with Mussolini's methods and political ideals, and was suspicious of him from the start, came away thinking of him as 'a master of men'.[11]

Esme returned with Isabella to England, where, between 1934 and 1936, often on visits to Lyulph's Tower, he worked hard to finish his autobiography. He died in August of 1939. In the period of mourning that followed, Hubert, and his brothers Francis and Mondi, were never far from their mother's side. In view of his father's long service to the country, Hubert, with great foresight, persuaded the Crown to grant his widowed mother a so-called 'grace-and-favour' apartment at the great Tudor palace of Hampton Court. This imposing building, dating from 1514, was originally home to Cardinal Wolsey, then Bishop of York, who was later obliged to make it over to his master King Henry VIII. In the seventeenth century, under William and Mary, the buildings were extensively redesigned, extended and furbished by Sir Christopher Wren. Early in the nineteenth century, Queen Victoria turned the palace into one of the finest historic museums and gardens in the country. 'The past is at least secure,' says an old American proverb and, indeed, some corners of the rambling building conserve the faint echoes and hauntings of Howard history, of courtly intrigue and indulgent living.

Since 1760, the palace had served, among other purposes, to provide apartments to the widows of worthy servants of Crown and country. There, the sweet, gentle, exemplary and always prayerful Isabella lived out her twenty-four years of widowhood in the frail but distinguished company of other elderly widows: of admirals, generals, politicians, diplomats, civil servants and courtiers. She had the use of a private garden, and more space than she needed. It was the perfect residence, and her sons and grandchildren went there often to visit her, and from her example and conversation to learn so much about what is valuable in life.

CHAPTER FIVE

Osasto Sisu and the Finnish Debacle

T HE story of Hubert's experience as a volunteer soldier in Finland, in 1940, has never been told. Although what happened can ultimately only be described as a debacle, it encapsulates Hubert's altruism, courage, patience and resourcefulness.

With the outbreak of war on 1 September 1939, sparked by the German invasion of Poland, Hubert began to mull over the possibility of moving from the Carnegie Foundation and joining the armed forces. Now thirty-one, however, he was too old for combat. He was refused a ground role with the Royal Air Force and it would have taken over a year to get into the Navy. He turned then to the Foreign Office, where he received three excellent offers, and, at his own request, joined the Northern European desk, starting on 11 January 1940. While Hubert's job proved responsible and satisfying, an opportunity arose that altered his course completely.

On 30 November 1939, in the tense atmosphere surrounding German aggression, the Soviet Union had made an unprovoked and widely condemned attack on neutral Finland. The United Kingdom made a promise to the League of Nations that it would do all it could to help resist the Russians. Hubert decided to volunteer for a British-led contingent, part of a larger international force, that would be sent as quickly as possible to aid the Finnish army. He saw this situation as a confrontation between right and wrong, and was probably influenced also by the fact that the

Russian action was condemned by Pope Pius XII, a personal friend of Hubert's mother.

One might wonder whether Hubert's decision to resign his post at the Foreign Office, leave his recently widowed mother in England and take a bold step into the unknown was intemperate, even foolhardy. And while the expedition turned out to be poorly managed, and inconsequential, Hubert's decision was based on his own reasonable political assessment, much of it made while he was working for the Carnegie Foundation in London. So well in touch was he with the evolving political scene in northern Europe that, the day after Christmas 1939, he penned a memorandum concerning Finland's conflict with the Russians. He put it like this:

> If events are allowed to take their normal course, there can be little doubt that Finland must ultimately be defeated … on the ground. The scales are very unevenly balanced. Russia has a population of approximately 180 million, almost unlimited natural resources and a big armaments industry. Against this, the population of Finland is only four million, the country is not endowed with any great natural wealth and depends for its materials of war almost entirely on foreign imports … If the Finns are to redress the overwhelming superiority of Russian manpower and resources, they will need more than courage. They will need active support from countries abroad.[1]

Echoes of his thinking appeared in the *Daily Telegraph and Morning Post*, on 23 January 1940, soon after he joined the Foreign Office:

> Reports from Europe to the Carnegie Endowment for International Peace stated that American aid is essential if Finland is to resist successfully the Russian invasion … It was pointed out that Britain was not in a position to give much help because she needed all the arms she could manufacture. One of the reports stated: 'The fact must not be concealed that, if Finland falls, Sweden will almost certainly fall also under German control.'[2]

Finnish troops on the move during the Winter War, 1939–40

THE INTERNATIONAL VOLUNTEER FORCE, as it was known, was recruited with commendable speed. In charge of the British contingent was a high-ranking committee, the Committee to Aid Finland, approved by the War Office and operating under the auspices of the Finnish Government. Its purpose was to superintend a newly formed agency, the Finnish Aid Bureau, which was opened at the end of January at Thorney House, in London's Smith Square. The British recruitment process got under way swiftly, attracting some 2,000 applicants, many of whom were sent home. In spite of good intentions, a combination of haste and poorly thought-out procedures resulted in the signing up of a man who had a wooden leg, another who had recently suffered from amnesia, two who were blind in one eye (one of whom said that having no left eye was not a problem as he was right-handed), another with curvature of the spine and another crippled with meningitis. One turned up saying he had come to fight the 'bloody Finns', several had minor criminal records; others were clearly too old because the age limit had been raised by agreement with the Finnish Government, to gain extra volunteers. It later became apparent that among those selected were a number of troublemakers, misfits and layabouts, in no way willing to pull their weight.

On 7 March 1940, Hubert innocently signed an agreement with the bureau – effectively, therefore, with the Finnish Government – to go to Finland. He was assigned the identification number 1076. Among the conditions of service was that the Committee to Aid Finland would undertake to supply Hubert with food, clothes and equipment during his period of service, and would pay him, as a volunteer initially with the rank of private soldier, from the date of enlistment to the date of demobilisation, the sum of two shillings a day. The last of the clauses in the agreement, importantly, provided this assurance: 'Except in the event of death, the Committee is bound to provide transport for the return of the volunteer to his place of enlistment.'

FINNISH AID BUREAU.

Conditions of Service and Form of Enlistment in the
International Volunteer Force for Finland.
BRITISH CONTINGENT.

Agreement

This Agreement is made on the ...Seventh.
day of ...March......19.4.0.: BETWEEN GEORG ACHATES GRIPENBERG, Envoy Extraordinary and Minister Plenipotentiary for Finland to the Court of St. James's acting on behalf of the Finnish Government, HAROLD GIBSON, the Director of the Committee of the FINNISH AID BUREAU of Thorney House, Smith Square, Westminster, as Agent and on behalf of the said Committee and ...Hubert John Howard............
(hereinafter called "the Volunteer").

1. The Volunteer agrees to enlist in the International Volunteer Force for Finland—British Contingent.

Hubert's Agreement with the Finnish Aid Bureau, dated 7 March 1940

Soon after volunteering, Hubert was approached by Kermit Roosevelt (1889–1943), someone he knew from his father's Washington days.[3] The young Roosevelt was a keen adventurer like his president father Theodore. Aged fifty at this time, he was already a hardened soldier, having won the Military Cross in Mesopotamia (now Iraq) during World War I. He had recently become a British subject (one imagines in order to gain the opportunity of more adventure) and was now an officer in the Middlesex Regiment. On 3 March, he was appointed commanding officer of all the British volunteers for Finland. On learning that Hubert was among them, Roosevelt asked him if he would be his aide-de-camp in Finland, and Hubert readily agreed, attracted by the idea of doing staff work on the front line. Roosevelt, however, fell ill shortly afterwards, and had to abandon the Finnish expedition altogether. He was later reinstated in his old regiment.

Hubert's reports and letters on the Finnish initiative were often directed to two former colleagues from the Carnegie Endowment, which had close ties with Columbia University in New York City. These were Dr Nicholas Murray Butler, the University's long-serving president, and Henry S. Haskell, a retired director. It is apparent that Hubert, for his insightful *in loco* reporting of the northern European war scene, received some continuing allowance from the endowment.

On 9 March, Hubert left London by train and on the following day boarded SS *Meteor* at Leith, Scotland, with the main British-led contingent, a total of 148 men. This was made up of three platoons and a headquarters group, to which Hubert was quickly assigned with the rank of sergeant. In command was Captain Douglas Holden Blew-Jones, appointed by Thorney House. His second in command was Lieutenant Joseph Joyce. In two black pocket notebooks, Hubert kept careful records of the events from the moment of embarkation.[4] His analysis of the situation is masterly, not only in terms of the volunteer force, but also in terms of the wider political context. They are also highly subjective, betraying a certain fatalism and a touch of the picaresque. There is irony, too, in the fact that Hubert – with his innate orderliness, his slightly dystopian vision, his background in diplomacy, his moral rectitude and common courtesy, and sheltered as he had been by the nature of his upbringing – should now find himself set adrift on the North Sea as part of a scratch military unit almost completely lacking in any form of discipline. This almost Sartrean nightmare somehow yielded its moments of situational humour in Hubert's wonderful observations of his fellow men. Of the hapless Blew-Jones, Hubert wrote:

> In appearance he was a dinosaur of a man, a pituitary giant who tempted one's thoughts back to the prehistoric age of a serene and predominantly vegetable existence. What he gained in stature [by means of his unexpected promotion] he lacked in vigorous attainment. He was good-natured, with a pleasant sense of humour; but if he was prepared to accept the title, he seemed unwilling to undertake the burden of his command. Such an amiable personality fell prey to the industry and intrigues of a small, ambitious and unscrupulous rascal.

Here he introduces the 'rascal', a certain Lieutenant Arthur Herbert Fraser, who craved power and usurped his position:

> So strong a hold indeed did Fraser establish over Blew-Jones, already from the second day of the journey on the boat, that a suspicion gained credence that he possessed either a peculiar attraction or an illegitimate lever over his so-domesticated superior officer. In the confusion which abounded on the ship at Leith, after its occupation by the volunteer contingent, Fraser skilfully inserted himself and his luggage in Blew-Jones' cabin. The bunk was indeed reserved for, and by preference should have been occupied by Lieutenant Joyce, who was second in command. While Blew-Jones fondly discovered in his baggage an impressive multiplication of strong intoxicants, Fraser set a guard about the cabin door and proceeded to give orders.

The journey was a nightmare, not because the seas ran high but because, in Hubert's words, of the 'disorder, the maladministration of funds and food, the destruction and appropriation of property and the growing discontent'. SS *Meteor*, sailing as part of a convoy, was bound for the port of Bergen, in neutral Norway. From there the plan was for the contingent to use Sweden as a stepping stone into Finland. The vessel was half a day out from Bergen when news reached the men of the Moscow Peace Treaty, signed on 12 March. This brought the so-called Winter War between Russia and Finland to a close. At a stroke, in theory at least, the entire expeditionary force became redundant. Hardened veterans of the gallant Finnish resistance to Russia wept at the news.

On arrival in Bergen, some men asked immediately to be repatriated. The Finnish Foreign Ministry insisted, however, that they expected further hostilities, that the Finnish Government had not yet ratified the Treaty (it did so the following day), and that the contingent should proceed to Lapua, in south Ostrobothnia 200 miles northwest of Helsinki, where other members of the British Expeditionary Force had already arrived. Hubert's contingent left Bergen by train on 16 March, and crossed into Finland via the twinned border towns of Haparanda on the Swedish side and Tornio in Finnish Lapland, on the northern tip of the Gulf of Bothnia. The frontier crossing was by foot, which Hubert, bearing in mind the extent to which discipline in his contingent had broken down even during the voyage to Bergen, described in his diary as a 'dishevelled march ... that may have resembled the retreat from Moscow without the spectacular appendage of a Napoleon'.[5]

The plan was to do six weeks' military training at Lapua, where there was an old barracks (last occupied by the Russians in 1917), and then move east to Savonlinna, closer to the Russian border. When the entire International Volunteer Force was counted on arrival in Lapua on 20 March, it consisted of 717 volunteers from twenty-two nations. Formed into several company units under the cover name *Osasto Sisu*, meaning 'the tough detachment', the British force numbered 155 men. On 27 March, there was a flurry of excitement when the legendary Field Marshal Carl Gustaf Emil Mannerheim (1867–1951), soldier, statesman and Commander-in-Chief of the entire Finnish army, arrived to welcome and inspect the volunteers. Mannerheim's reputation had preceded him. A former soldier in the Imperial Russian Army, he was fearless in battle, charismatic in character and decisive if somewhat eccentric. In Poland in 1914, he famously mounted a horse while naked and led his troops across a river at the height of winter. For Hubert, this visitation meant something more because his father, Esme, from his time as head of the British Legation in Stockholm, had come to know Mannerheim well.[6] The moment was brief, however, and on 30 March, Hubert, having appraised the situation and observed some of his fellow recruits, despatched a somewhat despairing letter to his friend Colville ('Collie') Barclay of the Foreign Office, responding to his request for a report. In it, Hubert expressed his frustration with the situation, while deploying his sense of humour and keen powers of observation:[7]

You hope no doubt to hear about war, and I certainly expected to be deeply involved in such an occupation. But I am overwhelmed by peace and can find time to write to you and other friends. In fact, the endless forest and the cloudless skies which surround this place give a sense of calm and stillness, and I escape from the barrack room in the afternoon and trek through the woods on skis, with a sense of awe, similar to that which I believe Russians get when they are sent to Siberia. The idea of war seems altogether ridiculous in this part of Finland now.

Life, of course, is far from normal, natural or pleasant. To begin with, the day starts at 6.00 a.m. One doesn't exactly feed in a trough, but one washes in one, conjuring from a frozen tap a reluctant stream of water. The greater problems of life are smothered by the trivial irritations of coarse woollen underwear, persistent rations of cheese and impolite language.

I think that if we stay here much longer, we may outstay our welcome. The gesture of coming is appreciated, but it is difficult to see what a purely military unit such as ours can now do to help Finland.

A group of volunteers is likely to contain an unusual assortment of men. Yet I can hardly imagine a stranger conglomeration than that which has gone to make up the British contingent. In emphasising the odd, I shall tend to give undue prominence to a comparatively small section of the whole. Probably about 75% are normal human beings, cheerful, youthful and long-suffering, who would make excellent material for a good army. Nevertheless, salt gives taste to porridge; and a teaspoon of vinegar can embitter the noblest vintage. It is natural and human on my part to take greater notice of the rarer elements. There is, for instance, T. Apostolides, a Scotsman from the Isle of Skye. Yet neither a brogue nor battle dress can conceal the atavistic impression of a Levantine monk. His forage cap sits embarrassed on a pinnacle of swarthy curls. There is the shy Mr Way, a personality who has become my friend. He wanders about intently looking for wisps of hay to send to his favourite mare at Newmarket, who is foaling. Besides his racing stables, he shows a quaint interest in runic stones. Creeping about in Eskimo boots and a leather jerkin is Prince Alphonse di Liguori, a Russian by extraction, who travels on an Italian passport and is settled in South Africa. He served in the Archangel Expedition [the brief Allied intervention in the Russian Civil War from 1918 to 1919] and hoped to do some useful work again, but his natural fatalism has broken down under the intolerable strain of the journey out, and he has recently been wandering around muttering to himself and fumbling a letter from General Ironside [who had commanded Allied forces in Northern Russia in World War I and was now Chief of the Imperial General Staff].

Blew-Jones and Fraser were dismissed almost immediately on arrival, Blew-Jones because he was incompetent, Fraser because he diverted the contingent's surplus money into his own account. The race was on for a new commanding officer. The first candidate was Joyce, the veteran soldier and second in command. He, although eclipsed on the voyage by the ambitious but corrupt Fraser, ignored the possibility, on arrival in Bergen, of aborting the expedition in the light of the armistice. As Hubert put it, 'Joyce was quickly, and indeed one might add mercifully, extinguished by a bronchial wheeze.'

The second candidate, a member of the Finnish army, was the Eton-educated but in Hubert's mind woefully inadequate Captain Hugo

Chandor. He, by a process of elimination and good fortune for himself, was nevertheless appointed to the job and was soon overwhelmed by requests for repatriation. About half the British contingent left against the better judgement of their superiors, just as the Germans started to invade Norway. It was now impossible to cross into Sweden by land. A number of those who fled on their own were eventually trapped in Norway; others ended up doing hard labour in German concentration camps. Several eventually got back to England, including the colourful Prince di Liguori.

The position for Hubert and the remainder of the British contingent was unenviable, complex and dangerous. Although they were to all intents and purposes redundant because of the peace treaty with Russia, they were entitled to be fed, and their Finnish Aid Bureau contract was accordingly extended to 31 May. The British Government continued to vacillate over repatriation, while the Finnish position hardened further. On no account could it permit the volunteers, as a unit or in groups, to cross the Finnish-Norwegian border. As Hubert put it in a letter, with resigned diplomatic sensitivity, 'such an act would be considered as un-neutral by Germany and could risk its [Finland's] delicate balance on the Russo-German tightrope for a handful of impatient Englishmen'.

As of 17 April, all the Osasto Sisu volunteers had been subsumed as expected by the Third Finnish Army Corps. The move to Savonlinna, where they arrived in the early hours of 18 April, integrated them as part of Finland's second line of military defence. The picturesque old town, on the east coast of Finland, is dominated by a centuries-old castle. Billeted initially inside the theatre-cum-ballroom of the Hotel Seurahuone, the British volunteers did their own catering, improvising with the basic Finnish army rations provided. They drilled and did route marches and weapons training. Even in April there was an occasional flurry of snow. The locals were deferential towards the British, occasionally bringing out a band to play for them or making available a ferry boat for a tour of the local islands and waterways. The Finnish army would turn up from time to time to share a new weapon or demonstrate their fieldcraft or battle techniques. Encouraging messages occasionally arrived from Mannerheim and from the Finnish Aid Bureau.

On 19 April, the bureau sent a formal note to Hubert's mother at Hampton Court Palace informing her that H. J. Howard (1076) 'was being useful' and was now in the Province of Savonlinna. This good news masked the fact that the men were again becoming restless. There was an outburst of complaints because the porridge one morning was served without milk or sugar and because the men disliked sausage sandwiches made with brown bread. Resentment simmered concerning Captain Chandor's intensification of their work regimes and the apparent aimlessness of their general situation. Lord Balfour of Burleigh, a senior member of the committee in London, visited the volunteers on 27 April, and made the position starkly clear: 'You came here to fight … It is quite possible the Russians may attack again.' Balfour had just met Mannerheim in Helsinki, who had repeated again that, in view of Finnish neutrality, the volunteers could not be transferred to Norway. So, for Hubert and his fellow volunteers, the northern port of Petsamo seemed the only exit route, but there was not a ship in sight.

On 4 May, Hubert was delegated by the men to warn the increasingly unpopular Chandor, who seemed to want the men to be rooted forever on Finnish soil, that a strike was imminent, which Hubert was then asked to forestall. He did so by organising an 'all-ranks' petition urging the powers that be to move them all up close to Petsamo for swift evacuation should a ship become available. Hubert presented this to Chandor on 7 May. Chandor reacted with fury, suggesting to Hubert that if he sent the petition to the bureau, Hubert himself might be accused of mutiny. Throughout the month, to rumours of evacuation was added further talk of such a mutiny, much of it exaggerated as if it were imminent. This exacerbated the tensions, even though Osasto Sisu was due to be formally disbanded at the end of the month and the men returned one way or another to civilian life. Several more now absconded out of sheer frustration.

As there was still no sign of an official move, Major Magill, British military attaché in Savonlinna, tried rallying the men on 30 May, the eve of their disbandment, in what he hoped would be a rousing speech. It was a disaster. He stressed that it was vital to keep the British name as good as possible in Finland, and for the volunteers not to disperse but to stay together. He hinted that many Finns were pro-German, but stated guardedly that each conscript was free to make up his own mind. He added that while there had been the possibility of the Admiralty laying on a ship to get them back to England, this was now almost impossible because Germany was aggressive and safety could not be guaranteed. Mindful, perhaps, of the bureau's 'contractual' pledge to get each volunteer home, he added, 'For God's sake, be persuaded that we are doing a lot to get you back.' At one point he referred to the men as 'a fine body of blackguards', which made matters worse.

The following day, two Orders of the Day were posted in the barrack room. Order Number 72 came directly from Field Marshal Mannerheim himself, in grandiose words that contrasted with the reality of the situation:

Field Marshal Carl Gustav Emil Mannerheim, Commander-in-Chief of all Finnish defence forces during World War II and later 6th President of Finland

British Volunteers,

Now that you are about to leave our country, I thank you who with high courage came to the aid of Finland in her fight for freedom and independence. Though fate denied you the opportunity of going into action, I wish to express to you my gratitude for your courage and enthusiasm in support of our cause. We in Finland will never forget you, who, at a time when your own country was in peril, hastened to our snowclad North, ready to lay down your lives in the cause of freedom. May the memories of your service in the Finnish army be happy ones, and may the future bring happiness and success to your own country.[8]

ON 1 JUNE, the contingent was formally demobilised and the men forbidden to wear uniform or carry any insignia. They were now to be incognito. A further sixteen of them left the party and made individual but unsuccessful attempts to get home. None had civilian clothing, some stole, others sold their uniforms for cash. To Hubert's dismay, discipline worsened once more. On 8 June, prompted by his acute sense of orderliness, Hubert wrote the following:

The barrack room is in a frightful state. The men laze about till 9 or 10 a.m. The noise at night up to midnight is appalling. I went in this evening and found men catapulting potatoes at each other. The CSM [Company Sergeant Major] came in during the afternoon today and asked, 'What about the football match?' Roome, who was supposed to organise it, was getting into his sleeping bag and yelled back, 'We are all too tired.' In fact, half the men were lying on their bunks. The demoralisation is complete and this is due to the fact that all discipline has gone.[9]

During the month of June, Hubert, now at least partially liberated, spent a good deal of time in Helsinki. Mannerheim invited him to a tête-à-tête lunch there one day, after which he introduced him to the head of the

Finnish secret services. These encounters may have helped move things along because the British Legation in Helsinki soon moved to disperse the remnant of the party to a number of locations, mostly in central or western parts of the country, where the men could find or be assigned work, stay out of sight and preferably out of trouble. The expatriate British colony in the capital also raised funds to help the stranded volunteers, who, in the perception of some, were in danger of becoming an embarrassment to Finland. Hubert, no doubt with some relief, moved from Savonlinna to Kauttua, close to the Gulf of Bothnia and northwest of Helsinki.

It was policy at the time for the Finnish authorities to employ stranded foreign volunteers, thus freeing up more Finns to join the regular army. Hubert quickly found work in one of the town's famed paper mills. His lodgings were better compared with those in Savonlinna, and his wages and daily volunteer allowance adequate. To exercise his mind, he taught English to employees of the company and they taught him Swedish, an official language of the Finns. As part of his work, but mainly because he had been advised to go into hiding from the Germans, Hubert spent prolonged periods in the forests, masquerading as a lumberjack, cutting timber and living in a wooden hut. He kept in touch with the authorities by means of a small radio transmitter. To his delight, he emerged from his hut one morning to find a wolf sitting a short distance from him. After work that evening, he scattered a few biscuits where the wolf had sat, and by the morning they were gone. On each successive evening, presumably until he ran out of biscuits, Hubert delighted in placing them closer and closer to the hut, to the point where an instinctive trust developed.[10] Hubert wrote that the experience alleviated his loneliness.

In August, Hubert wrote a long note to Henry Haskell in New York, which included comments about his experience of Finland:

> I find Finland an altogether delightful country. The endless woods and lakes have an atmosphere of peace about them, which I have not sensed anywhere else in the world. The people are very friendly and straightforward, not at all corrupted by modern usages though sometimes a little addicted to the more venerable inclinations of

drinking strong. They tend, men and women alike, to be well-built, and handsome, and their physical strength lends ease even to the most exacting labour, so workmen seldom give the impression of working hard, but it is difficult at any time to equal them. Their language would tax the intelligence even of a natural philologue, yet it is among the most beautiful languages I know to listen to.[11]

The theme of peace and peacefulness, and the adoption of an almost lyrical style of writing infused with a passion for nature, emerged strongly in his later writings about Finland. We find this in an extract from a letter to Anne Bazley, his future sister-in-law, five months after Hubert reached Stockholm:

It was a strange experience to go to a country with the expectation of being thrown into a desperate war, and then find oneself in an all-pervading peace. For peace in Finland is almost a physical thing which stretches with unbroken majesty over its endless sunlit woods and lakes. Even when the wind moves the tops of the trees, a powerful harmony like that of an organ in full blast, vibrates high above one's head among the swaying branches yet the boles [trunks] stand firm in their serried ranks, outdistancing the imagination, and the air between them is still.[12]

THE MONTHS passed. Hubert's personal records went quiet, although in diplomatic and government circles great efforts were being made to repatriate the volunteers – not just the rump of the British contingent but also men from other nationalities who had taken their chances in wartime Finland. Rationing was introduced. Only small quantities of butter, milk, jam and eggs were available, while fish was plentiful and became a more staple diet than usual in the absence of soup, meat and pudding. Owing to German blockades and the sinking of Finnish transatlantic ships, the country was completely cut off. Hubert, his patience sorely tested, could only resign himself to the situation. When winter came, he exercised by regular skiing, Nordic-style, in the snow-clad forests. He appreciated the isolation and the adventure. It is noticeable that the envelopes of his infrequent incoming mail had the words 'prisoner of war' handwritten on them, presumably to expedite delivery. Occasionally he wrote letters, one of which revealed the extent to which his morale had dropped in the space of just five months. It was addressed again to Henry Haskell in New York. In it, Hubert describes the situation as critical:

> We don't count for an atom here. An old tin can on a garbage heap in England is worth more than any of us. That is why, in the national interest as well as our own, I think it is best for us to support ourselves individually if we can. We keep quiet and we cease to be a burden, and our destiny has decided that this is the most, as well as the best, we can do. On the other hand, we can continue to prepare ourselves so that if at any time we are called upon to take a more active part in the struggle, we shall be ready to do so. It is not your fault or mine that we are here, apart from the fact that we chose to come out. But some of us saw clearly, as far back as Lapua, the necessity of getting out of Finland as soon as possible, and we urged it in every legitimate way. It is due to the miserable vanity and foolish infatuation of those who were responsible for us that we are still here. Against these, we have no redress now nor ever shall have.[13]

Within two months, Hubert had worked out an undisclosed means of reaching Stockholm. He wrote to Nicholas Butler in New York on 20 December, the eve of his departure from Kauttua. In his letter, he vaguely conjectured that if, in Sweden, he managed to obtain a visa from the Russians, he might travel east and join Sir Archibald Wavell's 'war machine' now confronting the Italian fascist army in North Africa.

He envisaged remaining with Wavell until the end of the war, fearing that the British Government would not let him go home any sooner. He wrote that getting a visa:

> will apparently depend on the pleasure of Madame Kolontey, the Russian minister in Stockholm. She has, I believe, a weakness for

extravagant clothes and very select society, which I shall find perplexing as I am apt to be a little impatient with extreme conservatism.

Hubert also related that the Germans, anxious to block the return of volunteers who might one day face the German army, had already set up a network of informers in Sweden, and how on a prior occasion he had drawn up an escape plan with one of the Swedish shipping companies.[14]

On the eve of his getaway, the German military attaché in Stockholm rang up the Finnish authorities to inform them of Hubert's plan. Hubert subsequently ascertained that there was a 'mole' in the office of the managing director of the shipping line and that, because of the unwillingness of the Swedes to stand up to the Germans, the man could not be dismissed. In the postscript to his letter, Hubert, seeking any imaginable solution to his problem, hinted at another possibility: that of working in Anglo-American relations in London and that, 'if this were suggested', the British Government might be tempted to get him home. Hubert's letter was overtaken by events as it did not reach New York until 5 February 1941.

Hubert finally left Kauttua. His diary reveals that he had been advised by the Finnish secret services, 'when and how to stow away on a Finnish ship'. We know only that he reached Stockholm on 21 December 1940, where he already had useful connections. To mark his departure, a friend, Roland Vessey (who also worked for the mill and was a farmer in civilian life) penned him a few lines of rather modest and, as it turned out, overly optimistic valedictory verse, in the manner of Wordsworth:

> Howard! Thou should be back in London now.
> England hath need of thee: for now our folk
> Are fighting for our homes, their lives; and how
> They bear the fire and bombing from the skies
> We midst these silent snows can scarce realise.

Go to the post that surely there awaits;
Bear them fresh strength in your far-seeing thoughts.
Go to your Western friends; swing wide their gates;
Spark through their pregnant power; unite their aims
To burn up evil in its own cruel flames.

When in the fight, be it with pen or sword,
Think of these quiet days 'mid snow and fire',
Where helpful thought displaced the idle word.
The ever-present power of silent prayer
Will take you safe to days more calm and fair.[15]

Hubert's decision to go to Sweden had been prompted by Malcolm Munthe, who, having already survived action in the Winter War, was serving at this precarious time as assistant military attaché at the British Legation in Stockholm.[16] Munthe, son of the well-known Swedish author and physician Axel Munthe, had been Hubert's friend since childhood and British Legation days, twenty-two years earlier. He was keenly familiar with the story of Osasto Sisu, knew Hubert's predicament, and advised him to seek work at the legation. The Foreign Office responded affirmatively and Hubert was soon employed there, reporting to the head of the legation, Victor Mallet.[17] As Hubert noted in a letter, 'It is a strange coincidence to find myself working in the house where I played as a child.'

The legation was at this time submitting a stream of daily visa applications to the Russians, who, so Hubert wrote, would put 'one hundred names into a top hat, shuffle them, draw out five and refuse the rest'. While Hubert had a busy desk at the legation, he was in effect now stuck in the Swedish capital, blocked by Russian bureaucratic ineptitude, the impotence of the neutral Swedish Government and the darkening shadow of a pan-European war. He remained in Sweden until summer 1942 when, finally, he was able to return to London on a British diplomatic flight.

CHAPTER SIX

Brothers at War

T	wo years had passed since Hubert had left London for Finland.
Even after his gruelling experiences, he was as determined as
ever to serve actively in the Allied war effort. Being half Italian,
and with many relatives in Italy, he and his brothers were affronted by the
fascist rise to power: by Mussolini's brutal invasions of Abyssinia and
Albania, his deferential collusion with the Germans and the escalating
German presence in Italy.

Hubert's first move was to return to the Foreign Office, this time to a
branch known as the Political Warfare Executive. In early 1943 he was
assigned, as was Mondi, to General Eisenhower's so-called Psychological
Warfare Branch (PWB), a secret outfit attached to his headquarters
for Operation Torch (the invasion of French North Africa and the
further invasions of Sicily and the Italian mainland). Its aims were the
accumulation of political intelligence: testing the vagaries and temperature
of public opinion in the occupied territories and, beyond the battle front,
using propaganda, including radio broadcasts and pamphleteering, to
support the Allied war effort up and down the peninsula.

The young men in PWB – Americans, British, soldiers and civilians –
had a tendency to make up the job as they went along. This applied
particularly to political intelligence, which was not formed into a separate
unit until the autumn of 1943, when it was designated 'D Section'. Hubert
and Mondi were both assigned to D Section, which was tasked with

weekly reporting to headquarters on the conditions in enemy-occupied Italy. In reality it was quite a loose-knit operation, characterised by some degree of improvisation and informality.

Hubert and Mondi were now in readiness to join the Italian campaign. Hubert's military training in Finland had been preparation enough. Mondi, after receiving basic training and following a period of stultifying boredom guarding the London docks, spent many months at Chiseldon military camp, near Swindon in Wiltshire, where large numbers of Allied troops were being trained and equipped to invade France. That was to happen in June 1944.

BEFORE ASSESSING Hubert and Mondi's time in Italy, it is appropriate to trace the military paths of their brothers, Francis and Henry. Francis left Cambridge University and worked between 1938 and 1939 in the legal profession; on the death of his father in 1939, he assumed the title of Baron Howard of Penrith. He joined the army as soon as the war started, aged thirty-three. After a period of tedium manning an anti-aircraft battery, he was promoted to captain. He then joined Commando 62, a secret unit of some fifty-five men, recruited and led by Captain Gus March-Phillipps, described by Francis as 'a romantic who looked back to the days of the Elizabethan adventurers like Drake and Raleigh'.[1] After a brave and successful raid against the Germans in Freetown, West Africa, March-Phillipps decided to attempt several such raids on German-occupied territory before enlarging the unit. Francis' first mission with Commando 62, on 2 September 1942, was code-named Operation Dryad. It was a flawless midnight assault on the Casquets Lighthouse, in the Channel near Alderney. Arriving in a high-speed craft, the commandos fulfilled their mission by capturing seven Germans (three in their pyjamas), and wrecking the strategically valuable lighthouse.

On 12 September 1942, Francis went on the second of these raids, codenamed Aquatint. With March-Phillipps again in command, a landing party of eleven men set out in a torpedo boat from Portsmouth. The aim was to test the defences and, if possible, neutralise several gun emplacements and enemy-occupied houses close to Sainte-Honorine-des-Pertes on the Normandy coast. They would do this by scaling some cliffs and attacking from behind. It was an exceptionally dark and foggy night. Two miles from the French coast near Barfleur, at about 11 p.m., the men transferred to a collapsible boat called a 'Goatley'. The unit landed further east than intended – in fact opposite Saint-Laurent-sur-Mer and on a wide beach later to gain notoriety as 'Omaha', during the Normandy landings of 1944. They waded ashore just after midnight. Francis was left to guard the Goatley.

As his fellow commandos disappeared into the sand dunes, small arms fire opened up. He saw the helmeted silhouette of German soldiers against the skyline and with his limited German understood that they were investigating a boat. Although a barking dog had apparently alerted them to the landing, Hitler's rage over the Casquets Lighthouse episode and the disastrous and costly Dieppe raid (just three weeks before Aquatint) meant that all German coastal units were on high alert. Francis fired a shot at the Germans to warn them off, and they in return lobbed a grenade in his general direction. Out to sea the torpedo boat, now visible under flares, almost took a direct hit from a mortar shell. Slightly damaged, it had no option but to raise anchor and retreat across the Channel to safety.

As the outnumbered commandos raced back to the Goatley, three of them were killed including March-Phillipps, shot as he entered the water. Francis took a bullet to his right leg, just below the knee. He dived into the water to swim away, shedding his equipment so as to remain buoyant. He was lucky enough to collide with the now upturned Goatley. On top of it sat André Desgranges, a Free French member of the raiding party. Together they drifted back to shore where Francis lost consciousness.

When he awoke, violently sick due to ingesting quantities of salt water, he was surrounded by Germans. As he and Desgranges were carted off to hospital in Caen, Desgranges shouted encouragingly to onlookers at the scene, 'Ne vous inquiétez pas, on reviendra!' ('Don't worry, we'll be back!'). Soon transferred to Germany, Francis made the most of life in a military prison hospital, making soft animals for children, such as pigs and elephants, and exercising his talent and imagination as a caricaturist. He was repatriated less than a year later, as part of a prisoner-of-war exchange.

As we have seen, Henry's wartime experience began sooner than that of his brothers and in its first phase led him along an entirely different path. After his success at the Royal Military Academy at Sandhurst, his commission into the Coldstream Guards and his two years with the Somali Camel Corps, the desk job in London was uninteresting to him. As soon as World War II was declared, and with the war in North Africa escalating, he was ordered to take a troop of the King's African Rifles to

Hubert's younger brother Henry, as a senior under-officer
at Sandhurst Military Academy, c. December 1932

the Middle East to join the British Eighth Army under Field Marshal Auchinleck.[2] Henry was then sent to Cyprus where, in June 1941, he raised a volunteer commando to resist the invasion of the island by the Germans, which was expected after the fall of Crete. After Cyprus, he saw service with the Somalia Gendarmerie between September 1941 and May 1942 before returning to the Coldstreams for action in Egypt's Western Desert.

In 1943, worryingly, Henry contracted double pneumonia. A series of painful procedures left him badly scarred and his condition became critical. It must have been bad because his wife Adèle received a telegram in America containing the woefully exaggerated (but quickly remedied) news that her husband had died. Henry was invalided for a while and ended up in a Cairo hospital. Once fully recovered, he joined the Italian campaign in March 1944.

HUBERT AND MONDI arrived in Sicily in September 1943, two months after the Allies. Five months earlier, the corpse of an unfortunate tramp had been planted by a British submarine in the sea off the southwest coast of Spain, and picked up by local fishermen. He was dressed as a British naval officer and carried forged documents designed to trick the Germans into believing the Allied invasion of southern Europe would take place via Greece. The Germans therefore reinforced their defences in Greece so that in July 1943, when the Allies first landed in Sicily (in what was known as Operation Husky), the occupiers were quickly overwhelmed. During his short time on the island, Hubert assisted the American sociologist and educator Stuart Carter Dodd in organising a critically important opinion survey for the Allied forces in Sicily, the first ever of its kind in Europe.[3]

The mainland campaign against the German occupiers was launched by the Fifteenth Army Group, under General Harold Alexander, on 3 September.[4] The principal landings were on three fronts: at Salerno, south of Naples, with a force led by the American Fifth Army; at Reggio Calabria, on the toe of Italy, in what was essentially a British Eighth Army support operation; and at Taranto, to the east. The Italian armistice was officially declared five days later.

After reaching the mainland, Hubert and Mondi were stationed in Bari, from where they maintained contact with the British Eighth Army while trying to make sense of the bewildering factionalism that had broken out after the Italian capitulation on 8 September. Their specific assignments within the newly formed D Section differed, with the result that they met only occasionally. The brothers, and their growing number of colleagues, had to negotiate with fascists, communists, bona fide democrats, royalists (many with scarcely disguised fascist sympathies), and a wide range of Italian Co-belligerent Army groups and conscripts. Each non-fascist political group, jostling for political power once the war was over, was to an extent suspicious of their Allied 'partners' although the majority of Italians seemed, according to Mondi's diary, to be more fearful of Russian militant atheism than of homegrown fascism.

In November 1943, suitable headquarters for D Section were found in Naples. The address was 7 Viale Calascione. It was a fine three-level apartment once occupied by an ultra-fascist family but most recently by a disbanding group of Italians, sympathetic to the Allied cause, who had been working in undercover operations. Most of D Section moved there that month. Mondi installed himself in some splendour and Hubert called in when he could, and stayed there from time to time. Hubert's diaries, as indeed the letters he wrote to his mother and relatives, reveal little of his precise movements prior to the liberation of Rome, added to which PWB's classified records were substantially dispersed or destroyed after the war.

Mondi's war diary, however, records several encounters with Hubert. On Sunday 19 March 1944 – just three months before the liberation of Rome – they drove together to Salerno, where Hubert was due to cover the congress of the Christian Democrat Union. Hubert had apparently had trouble finding where it would take place as the venue had been moved without warning from the Teatro Verdi to some obscure seminary. He nevertheless found the proceedings interesting. After a long morning session on that first day of the congress, the brothers went in search of lunch together, travelling the exquisite coast road to Ravello – where they discovered that all the hotels had been requisitioned by the military. By early afternoon they had still found nowhere to eat. This ominous situation was resolved by an understanding policeman. He entrusted them to a small boy who led them down a back alley and out onto a huge balcony where food was produced for them. From there, as Mondi described it, they had one of the 'loveliest views in existence'. Returning to Naples that evening they saw Vesuvius 'flaming wildly', as Mondi put it, 'and throwing out masses of incandescent rock, while large steam clouds above the cone reflected the red glare. Down the mountainsides were streaks of glowing red, the beginning of a great lava flow'.

Four days later, on 23 March, Hubert and Mondi were summoned to a high-level meeting at the Allied headquarters in Caserta, some seventeen miles north of Naples. Central to the talks that day were two distinguished American military commanders. The first was Major General Harry Johnson, shortly to be appointed military governor of Rome. The second was Major General Edgar Hume, the most senior medical officer in the American army. After lengthy briefings by the brothers, Johnson asked them what they had been doing in civilian life before the war. Hubert said he had been the European representative of the Carnegie Institute for International Affairs, based in London. 'Well fancy that,' said Johnson. 'Here's old Andrew Carnegie leaves Scotland to make a big pile of money in the USA and here's this Britisher who helps him spend it back in the mother country!'

Hubert and Mondi met again on 11 April. It is a measure of the ease with which they mingled with the figureheads of the former Italian resistance in exile, that their supper guests for this D Section dinner in Viale Calascione were Carlo Sforza and Alberto Tarchiani.[5] Sforza's sculptor son, Sforza-Galeazzo, nicknamed 'Sforzino', was also there. It can only have been the five of them because just two chickens were consumed, accompanied by pasta and artichokes. Given that this was wartime, the Howards considered it a feast and joked that the lira 1,871 bill, equivalent to less than £5 today, was excessive. This intriguing and quite intimate supper party is neatly encapsulated, with occasionally humorous touches, in Mondi's war diary:

I was surprised by Tarchiani whom I sat next to during the feast. I did not expect him to be charming and found he was. He has an immense enjoyment of a joke and a pleasant, whole-hearted cackle. He likes inventing jokes and imagining absurdities. He may be a bit vinegary in politics but he is a pleasant companion. Sforzino, very handsome, rather effete, not talkative, sat opposite, occasionally making some rather acid remark. Carlo Sforza himself was magnificently effusive, whether recalling his remarks to Kaiser Wilhelm II about the bastardy of his branch of the Sforza family, or inveighing against the communists who have stolen all the heat from his fire, or making political aphorisms. He spoke with lordly condescension, draped like some expensive cloth over his chair. He can be very amusing in a lofty way and he can be charming. He can also be neatly venomous.

Mondi concluded his vignette of this amicable and fascinating *soirée politique* with the following:

Hubert told a very long, very amusing story about Goering being sent to Holland to raise morale and having a tremendous success because he was mistaken for Queen Wilhelmina... He told it in his rather slow, precise, very correct Italian. It was a delightful experience to listen to him. The whole company listened to him as if spell-bound. They laughed a lot in the middle when he described how Goering dressed up for the trip and most uproariously at the end, but between the middle and the end they listened with complete and silent attention so that the final outburst was terrific.

On 4 June 1944, Allied troops liberated Rome after intense fighting at Monte Cassino and in and around Cisterna, so close to Ninfa. Hubert and Mondi, being able to speak Italian, were among the first D Section officers to enter the capital. There, in spite of their intense military duties, they were able to take time off to visit their Giustiniani Bandini relatives. Mondi and his friend John Vernon soon managed to find and requisition a new headquarters for D Section: a spacious and run-down villa situated at 27 Via Po.[6] At different times it had been occupied by the German SS and the Gestapo. The writer and war correspondent Bernard Wall was among those who billeted there.[7] Long after the war, he gave a fascinating account of how, under the leadership of Ian Greenlees, 27 Via Po became something akin to a political and intellectual salon.[8] Here is a passage:

> We sat at that table in the room filled with the smoke of Toscano cigars. We who talked and argued about Italy's future until midnight and later like characters in a novel by Turgenev. We didn't make nationalistic divisions among ourselves; we were Englishmen and Americans who had known Italy and Italians before the war. Among those who lived in the house on the Via Po were Ian Greenlees, […] the two Howard brothers (one of whom [Mondi] later became Consul General in Genoa), and me. There were others who came from time to time. But what made the mess extraordinary was the list of guests we had to dinner. All the heads of parties came … Sforza was a frequent guest. There were also a number of writers and artists among our regular guests including Alberto Moravia, Elsa Morante, Mario Soldati, Emilio Cecchi … and many others. I remember a night when Umberto Saba and Giuseppe Ungaretti saw each other for the first time in many years.[9]

The Germans had now fallen back to their next significant line of defence, the Arno Line. Along this they held much of the city of Florence, and had created defensive positions in Fiesole and the surrounding hills, north of the Arno. The German-speaking Hubert, with his natural diplomacy and clear understanding of the political nuances at play, was deeply mindful of the need to save Florence from unnecessary damage, and played a key part in the multilateral negotiations that were to follow. He was quickly sent forward, to make contact with the partisans and the Florence Committee of Liberation. This committee was a subset of the highly organised Committee of National Liberation, formed soon after Italy's entry into the war on the side of the Allies, with responsibility for coordinating the Italian political and militaristic resistance in German-occupied territory. It consisted of leading patriots representing every shade of Italian political persuasion.

The distinguished anti-fascist Piero Calamandrei asked Hubert, on the tenth anniversary of the liberation of Florence, to write down his account of those dramatic days. This appeared in full in the September 1954 edition of Calamandrei's review *Il Ponte*.[10] Hubert recalled that Allied forces entered the outskirts of Florence from the south, on 4 August 1944, and that he followed the advance guard by way of Certosa, Poggio Imperiale and the Porta Romana. The atmosphere was feverish, with the long-suffering Italian civilians overwhelming the Allied troops and armoured columns with their expressions of gratitude, relief and joy. To Hubert it appeared like a victory parade, though he knew this to be premature. Early that first day, Hubert sat down on a hill somewhere between Val di Pesa and the Val d'Arno, and, with his PWB colleagues, studied maps and received radio briefings. It was a fine summer morning, with some ground mist. Behind them the dead and wounded from previous days' fighting were being taken into a small colonnaded church. Already there was tension, in anticipation of imminent orders to advance again so as to maintain pressure on the Germans.

On his way down from the Porta Romana, Hubert ran into junior members of the Florence Committee of Liberation – with just enough time for a handshake, brief expressions of solidarity and the promise of meeting up later. The partisan headquarters, in Piazza Santo Spirito, were less than a mile south of the Ponte Vecchio and in the Oltrarno quarter of Florence, close to the Palazzo Pitti and the Boboli Gardens. On the other side of the river, the north side, was the city centre which Hubert and his colleagues would have to reach in order to negotiate with the senior leaders of the committee, apparently holed up in the city hall pretending to be fascists.

On his first day in the Oltrarno, Hubert ran into the legendary partisan leader Aligi Barducci, head of the Garibaldi-Arno division. His *nom de guerre* was 'Il Potente'. Barducci's men were busy securing the southern side of the river, where German rearguard snipers still remained. Hubert's

principal mission, to cross into the city centre and to report back to the
Allies on the presence or otherwise of enemy fighters, was complicated.
Before their retreat to the other side of Florence, and during the night of
4 August, the Germans had systematically destroyed all the major bridges
of the Arno, with the exception of the Ponte Vecchio, whose shops they
had already mined and booby-trapped. Indeed, much of the Lungarno
Soderini had been pulverised, leaving mountains of rubble. To prepare
for the crossing, Hubert commandeered a jeep and, under the protection
of two tanks, drove cautiously along the old walls of the city via the Viale
Petrarca, San Frediano and the Lungarno Soderini. At this point they
were shot at from somewhere in the Bellosguardo, on their own side of
the river, prompting Barducci and his men to intensify their hunt for
enemy snipers east of the Oltrarno quarter.

General Alexander, in overall charge of this operation, unexpectedly
made a decision to withdraw his forces from the southern part of Florence
and to thrust northward in a flanking movement, avoiding fighting in the
historic centre. The situation was critical because the centre of Florence,
under curfew and cut off because of the fighting, was without transport,
water and provisions. News of this tactical withdrawal was greeted by
citizens and partisans alike with utter dismay. It seemed like hesitation
in the face of victory. Hubert and his comrades faced incredulity as well
as accusation. Although Hubert explained to the partisans that there was
to be a retreat, he and the PWB party were under army orders not to
hint at the underlying reasons. Things were by now extremely sensitive.

Over the next days, the Oltrarno and the rest of Florence's southern
quarters were successfully cleared of German snipers. On the evening
of 8 August, Hubert went up to Piazza Santo Spirito, which was full of
fighters mobilising for the next phase. There were civilians too. Without
warning, a German mortar round fell on the piazza. Barducci, standing
several yards away from Hubert, was mortally wounded, along with one
of Hubert's liaison officer friends; Barducci died the next day. There were
many injured. Hubert never had any doubt that the Germans had been
tipped off. He was reported to have been deeply upset by Barducci's death,
feeling he had become in some way bonded with a courageous fighter.

The partisans now needed urgently to get a contingent up to Monte Morello, two miles northwest of Florence, where some of their fighters had become trapped by the enemy. Their most direct route, now that the Germans had mostly evacuated the city centre, would be by crossing the river and advancing through the city as the crow flies. Against the wishes of the Allies, who wanted the city centre kept clear for two more days, the partisans decided to leave the next day. Hubert and one or two other PWB officers, needing to report on conditions in the city centre and liaise with the senior partisans, asked if they might cross the river with them. This was agreed.

At dawn on 9 August, the formation set off in single file, and, having negotiated the mines and the piles of rubble along the Lungarno Soderini, made for the diagonal dam known as the Pescaia di Santa Rosa, that lies between the Ponte alla Carraia and the Ponte della Vittoria. The dam was damaged in places and, although the summer water levels were quite low, the men were up to their knees in water and the current felt strong. As they crossed, in itself tricky, they knew they were at risk from German rearguard sniper fire.

Fortunately, there were no signs of the enemy on the other side. The partisan troop now headed northwest through the city towards Monte Morello, while Hubert and his two companions turned due east towards Piazza della Signoria – passing through Via del Parione, Piazza Santa Trinità, Via delle Terme and Porta Santa Maria. The darkness of the narrow medieval streets added to a sense of foreboding. The palazzi and the houses were as if fortified, shutters closed. In Hubert's description:

> As we advanced, I noticed that some of the blinds had been raised a few centimetres, and I felt hundreds of eyes fixed intensely upon me. What possible impression could this first small group of English officers, entering Florence unaccompanied and virtually unarmed, have made? And then we heard a strange and miraculous sound, probably never to be heard again. Hundreds of hands were now clapping us, and we could hear muffled voices of welcome and approval from our invisible observers.

Moments later they burst out into the 'sunlit splendour of Piazza della Signoria, with its magnificent tower, its fountains and its statues, and Michelangelo's David'. Hubert observed that the famous square 'had seen some of the most terrible and dramatic events in the history of Florence, but today it conveyed a wonderful sense of space, of freedom and light'. The centre of the city was not officially freed until 11 August 1944, two days later.

IN SEPTEMBER 1944 Mondi, John Vernon and Major Ivor Manley, a senior colleague from D Section, were transferred from Rome to Apulia, there to prepare for a parachute drop behind the new enemy line, along the Po Valley, in the north: the Gothic Line. (When it came to it, the following spring, the parachute operation never materialised as conditions were deemed too hazardous.) On 12 November, after further delay in Monopoli and Castellana, Mondi returned to Rome, there reuniting with his D Section comrades. Through John Vernon, he got to know the American servicewoman Jane McLean. Mondi speculated in his war diary: 'If I were an accomplished matchmaker, I'd see to it she married Hubert, but as my chief aim would probably be to acquire her as a sister-in-law, I think I had better not interfere.'[11]

Mondi spent the last months of the Italian campaign in Florence. As soon as the Gothic Line was smashed, he made his way to Milan where he arrived in a commandeered taxi on 30 April 1945, just after the execution of Mussolini and a few days before the German surrender in Italy on 2 May. World War II in Europe came officially to an end six days later, but Mondi was not demobilised until October as there was still so much work to be done.

HENRY HOWARD, having arrived in Italy in March 1944 after his discharge from the hospital in Cairo, was disappointed not to be able to rejoin the Coldstreams. His new role, as general staff officer (liaison) within the British mission to the Italian Co-belligerent Army, was nevertheless perfect for him in view of his fine military record, his seniority and fluent Italian. For the most part Henry remained in the south – Puglia, Campania, Lucania and Calabria – where Mondi and Hubert were already operating. His footsteps can be traced to Lecce, Positano, Catanzaro, Sila, Agrigento and Segesta. He seldom met his brothers during this period. Some surmise that Henry's highly classified role was to liaise not only with the regular Italian military under Allied control but also with the partisans who were operating extensively behind enemy lines. There is evidence he had a hand in trying to resolve the anti-draft rebellion by Sicilian anarchists that was centred in the town of Ragusa and which lasted throughout 1945. Eventually Henry moved northwards to Como and Venice, stopping at Fiastra where he called on his Giustiniani Bandini relatives. For his actions in Italy, the *colonello inglese* (as Henry was known to the Italians) was mentioned in despatches. Henry remained on special assignment in Italy until July 1945.[12]

AFTER THE German withdrawal to their Gothic Line, Hubert remained in Florence for some months – briefing, coordinating, and writing reports (including his weekly information letter). By this time, D Section was operative in Trieste, from where Hubert's colleague Ivor Manley corresponded regularly with him, issuing instructions and warnings about infiltrators, spies and enemy collaborators. Hubert was given leave of absence to return to England, which he did just after Christmas 1944. There he visited his mother and other relatives, and checked that things were in order at Lyulph's Tower. He returned to Italy in mid-March 1945, resuming military duties with assignments that took him back and forth between Rome, Naples, Florence and Milan. He returned to England on 17 August 1945, the war finally behind him.[13]

CHAPTER SEVEN

Hubert and Lelia

A FTER his repatriation, Hubert was without a civilian job. However, in addition to French and Italian, he spoke German quite fluently and had many contacts among Catholics in Europe. This enabled him to find work for a while in Germany, as a Catholic consultant within the Religious Affairs Branch of the Control Commission for Germany. His work there was essentially to help develop a theology of reconciliation between the Church of England and the Lutheran Church.

With this brief assignment over, Hubert returned to England and spent a period with his mother at Hampton Court Palace. He found her well, although she had been in some danger. Living to the southwest of London had been riskier than expected, with German V2 rockets passing overhead between September 1944 and April 1945, on their way to central London. These rockets, a last-ditch effort by the Luftwaffe to terrorise British citizens and turn the tide of the war, were to some limited extent thwarted by a cat belonging to Isabella's cook, which appeared to have extra-sensory perception. Whenever a rocket approached, the cat hid itself and so gave early warning to members of the household. One of these random and deadly bombs fell one night in nearby Bushy Park, sending shock waves through the palace.

Hubert soon returned north to his beloved Lyulph's Tower. Now that he could plan for the future, he acquired a small herd of dairy cows which he milked daily by himself, putting them to grass in the meadows down by the lake. While the dream itself was idyllic in some ways, the cost of this venture was such that Hubert could not afford any help. He struggled on for three years, socialising with his Howard cousins who lived in the vicinity, and adding his name to the membership of the Ullswater Preservation Society.

Lelia Calista Ada Caetani (b. 1913) was never far from Hubert's mind after his first meeting with her before the war. It helps to recall how this came about. Ties of friendship between his family and hers, directly or indirectly, long preceded their first encounter. These can be traced back to two other families who became linked through marriage to the Caetani. The first of these, whom the Howards knew well over several generations, was the English Bootle-Wilbraham family. Among the grandchildren of Edward, 1st Baron Skelmersdale, was Ada Bootle-Wilbraham.[1] This tall, striking and adventurous young woman met Onorato Caetani, 14th Duke of Sermoneta, during one of his many visits to London.[2]

They married in 1867, when she was just twenty. They had five sons and one daughter. Among these were Leone, the scholarly fifteenth duke, who abandoned Italian politics and emigrated to Canada;[3] Roffredo, the seventeenth and last Duke of Sermoneta, a fine composer who married the American heiress Marguerite Chapin;[4] and Gelasio, engineer, diplomat, and the visionary behind two extraordinary reclamation projects: the clearance of the ruined town of Ninfa, on whose site he and his mother laid out a garden that was to become internationally acclaimed, and the draining of the Pontine Marshes that, over the centuries, even the Romans and a succession of popes had failed to accomplish.[5]

Although Gelasio Caetani and Esme Howard came to know one another during the 1920s, as ambassadors to Washington for their respective countries, Esme had been absorbed quickly into the Caetani circle in 1886 during his first diplomatic assignment to Rome. From then on, he had been a regular guest of Ada and Onorato, who would invite

Ada Bootle-Wilbraham, Lelia's grandmother

him to their Rome parties and even to go rough shooting in their Pontine marshlands near Ninfa. From Esme's autobiography, we gain some flavour of that happy friendship:

> In those days nearly the whole area of the Pontine Marshes and their sea coast – something, I believe, like forty or fifty miles in length, and perhaps fifteen to twenty miles across – belonged to the Duke of Sermoneta. The duchess ... who was one of the great beauties of Rome, was a Miss Wilbraham and a sister of Mrs Kennedy, the wife of ... the counsellor of the embassy. The Kennedys were most kind to me and through them I got to know the Sermonetas well, and was allowed by the duke, when I went down to shoot, to stay for a night or two in his large palazzo in the little town of Cisterna ... a sort of capital of the Marsh district.[6]

Onorato Caetani, Lelia's grandfather, *c.* 1910

He goes on to describe the rigours of an overnight stay at the palazzo:

> I have seldom slept in a more ghostly place. It was almost devoid of
> furniture; my bedroom, I remember, was about as large and as high as
> the largest salon of the Royal Academy; there was in it an iron bedstead,
> a deal [wood] table and one chair; the floor, of course, was of brick and
> the walls were whitewashed. There was also what used to be called a
> *scendiletto*, or a [small] rug on one side of the bed. The only light in this
> vast room was a candle in a small candlestick. I had no notion where
> my nearest neighbour was in the great house, or indeed whether there
> was one, though I believe there was a *guardiano* who slept somewhere.
> My youthful imagination was fired by stories of the Italian Middle
> Ages and, as the candle flickered in the draughts which floated into this
> large and unheated room on a winter night, my mind's eye peopled the

Coat of arms of the Howard Dukes of Norfolk

Esme Howard's tapestry of the coat, now on
display in the Caetani Castle at Sermoneta

I

Thomas Howard,
3rd Duke of Norfolk,
by Hans Holbein, c. 1539

Thomas Howard,
4th Duke of Norfolk,
after Hans Eworth, c. 1563

II

St Philip Howard, Earl of Arundel, aged eighteen.
Portrait attributed to George Gower, 1575

Lyulph's Tower as it would have appeared to Wordsworth
and Coleridge when they first saw it in 1799

ENGRAVING PUBLISHED IN 1815 FROM A DRAWING BY JOSEPH FARINGTON, RA

Ullswater viewed from above Lyulph's Tower

The Bandini Castle, or Rocca, of Lanciano, the Marche

Lanciano Castle's ornate Salone Antinori

Charlotte Long,
Hubert's grandmother,
by Tito Conti, *c.* 1886

Esme, Lord Howard
of Penrith, by Henry
Harris Brown, *c.* 1931

'Tutti quanti' ('All of us'), Stockholm, c. 1916
Clockwise from top: Esme Howard, Hubert, Mondi,
Esmetto, Francis. Centre: Isabella with baby Henry

VII

Sir Esme Howard
H.M's Ambassador to Spain 1919

Portraits of Hubert's parents in their ambassadorial prime, from Esme's
two-volume autobiography *Theatre of Life*, published in 1935–6

VIII

Photo: Harris & Ewing, Washington

Isabella Howard
Washington. 1925.

IX

Hubert's red-ink letter to Francis concerning his tastes in music, dated 3 March 1924

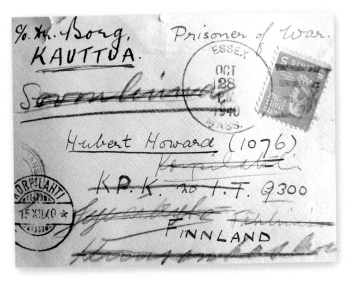

Redirected envelope addressed to Hubert as 'Prisoner of War'
and postmarked Essex, Massachusetts, 28 October 1940

'A group of volunteers is likely to contain an unusual assortment of men.'

Hubert (kneeling, to right of central gunner) with his company's machine gun unit, Savonlinna, Finland, May 1940

Ninfa's castle and tower and, beyond, the old municipal building

Inside the courtyard of the Caetani Castle at Sermoneta, and
the original private entrance to the garden at Ninfa

A luxuriant stretch of the river at Ninfa

The rock garden at Ninfa, one of Hubert and Lelia's special
gardening places, and Roffredo Caetani's 'sonorous' waterfalls

XIII

André Derain's portrait of Lelia when she was twenty-three, Paris, 1926

Lelia's painting of Hubert sitting at his desk at Ninfa, *c.* 1975

Lelia sketching from the battlements of the Caetani Castle
at Sermoneta (in the distance is Monte Circeo)

Hubert with Diane Kacich (later Howard) on Monte Semprevisa, Easter 1978

XVI

Roffredo Caetani, Lelia's father, *c.* 1910

place with ghosts of those who had probably had their eyes gouged out, or their fingernails extracted by some medieval ancestor of the duke. Antonio used to call me before dawn and I was always ready to start at the earliest possible hour in order to get away from the room thus haunted by my imagination.[7]

The second of these family ties came about through the aforementioned marriage in 1937 of Hubert's youngest brother, Henry, to Adèle Le Bourgeois Alsop, whose mother, Julia Chapin, was a first cousin of Marguerite. It was this, specifically, that led to Hubert's first meeting with Lelia, believed to have taken place in London, probably in 1936 or 1937, upon an introduction made by the newly engaged couple, Henry and Adèle.

BASED ON that providential introduction, and as soon as Florence was liberated, Hubert broke away from his military duties with PWB's D Section, and went alone to Ninfa on 1 November 1944. There is no way of telling whether, on that occasion, there was any spark of romance

Lelia on the knee of her mother Marguerite, *c.* 1913

between him and Lelia. Hubert is next recorded as having been a guest there on 1 April 1945, just a month before the German surrender in Italy. The occasion was a lunch party for twenty. Among Roffredo and Marguerite's guests were two veterans of wartime life at the Vatican, Sir D'Arcy Osborne, Britain's emissary to the Holy See, and Harold Tittmann Jr, appointed by President Franklin D. Roosevelt as America's papal envoy, in effect chargés d'affaires.[8] Both had become close friends of the Caetani, both were effectively trapped inside the Vatican for the duration of the war and both were closely in touch with the resistance and working hard to hide and, where possible, facilitate the escape of fugitive Jews and Allied servicemen.

Hubert brought with him on that spring day the affable British army officer Major General Langley Browning, who had expressed to him his love of trout fishing, the season for which had only just begun. (Although it was said that Roffredo was known on occasion to disoblige less-welcome fishermen by disturbing the water at the head of the river so as to drive the trout downstream and beyond reach, the sport on that day must have been a success because Browning was invited back to Ninfa to fish on at least six further occasions.)

Hubert's brother Henry, who, after several years of fighting in North Africa, had arrived in Italy in March 1944 as part of the Allied Military Mission to the Italian army, stayed overnight at Ninfa on 11 July. It is probable, as he knew Lelia well through his Chapin connections, that on this occasion he would have picked up from her some expression of her feelings for Hubert because, less than a week later, on 17 July, Hubert was back at Ninfa. Significantly, perhaps, there was just one other guest that day.

Back in England, Hubert spent a happy family Christmas (1945) in Gloucestershire with Francis and Anne Howard, his brother and sister-in-law, and with his mother and other members of the family. On New Year's Eve, from the Travellers Club on London's Pall Mall, he penned a letter to Lelia. His hopes that he and Lelia might meet again soon are expressed with due formality. However, in his reference to Lelia's dog, he charmingly reveals something of his often-quirky humour:

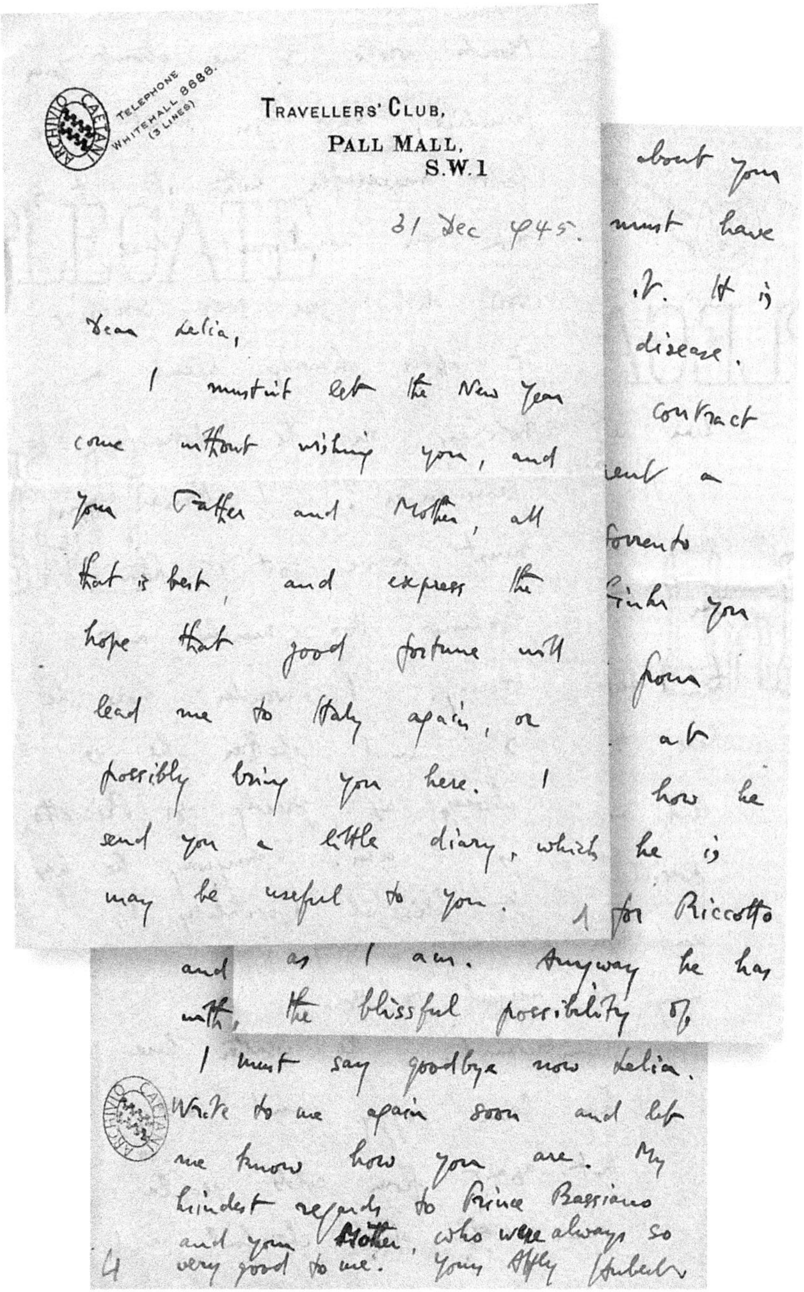

ARCHIVIO CAETANI

TELEPHONE
WHITEHALL 8688.
(3 LINES)

TRAVELLERS' CLUB,
PALL MALL,
S.W.1

31 Dec 945.

Dear Lelia,

I mustn't let the New Year come without wishing you, and your Father and Mother, all that is best, and express the hope that good fortune will lead me to Italy again, or possibly bring you here. I send you a little diary, which may be useful to you.

about you
must have
.N. It is
disease.
contract
ient a
Sorrento
Girls you
from
at
how he
he is
for Riccotto
and as I am. Anyway he has
with, the blissful possibility of

I must say goodbye now Lelia. Write to me again soon and let me know how you are. My kindest regards to Prince Bassiano and your Mother, who were always so very good to me. Yours Affly Hubert

4

Hubert's letter to Lelia, New Year's Eve 1945

I mustn't let the New Year come without wishing you, and your Father and Mother, all that is best, and express the hope that good fortune will lead me to Italy again, or possibly bring you here ... Mondi wrote to me about your jaundice, and you must have felt miserable with it ... I think you must have got it from looking too much at Honey [Lelia's dog]. I wonder how he is, and whether he is always as greedy for Riccotto [*sic*] as I am ... I must say goodbye now Lelia. Write to me again soon and let me know how you are. My kindest regards to Prince Bassiano and your Mother, who were always so good to me.[9]

On his several visits to Rome in the aftermath of the war, primarily to see his Giustiniani Bandini relatives, Hubert turned for hospitality to Mondi and Cécile, his brother and sister-in-law. Within months of his leaving the army, in late 1945, the Foreign Office had asked Mondi to move to Turin to set up an embryo consulate in the form of a small information and press office. From there, in June 1947, he had been transferred to Rome as political and legal counsellor at the British Embassy. Roffredo and Marguerite Caetani soon took Mondi and Cécile under their wing, inviting them on a number of occasions and being entertained in return. More than that, Roffredo offered them the top apartment of the Palazzo Caetani, into which they moved in April 1948.

Hubert and Lelia remained steadfastly in touch even though Marguerite began to worry that things between them were not moving along fast enough, and that Hubert might be dragging his feet. In August 1947 she and Lelia spent a few days touring England, and in Cumberland lodged near the Tower to ensure they were able to see Hubert and, with him, get to know some of the other Cumberland Howards. It was not, however, until 1949 that the romance reached a turning point. Cécile's diary records that Hubert, accompanying his mother, came out from London to stay on 20 January, and that on 24 January he went to Ninfa on his own for two nights to meet Lelia and her parents in the hope of becoming engaged. There was no other guest and Hubert returned to Palazzo Caetani two days later in a state of enormous happiness.

There was no fanfare to mark the engagement. It was a low-key affair, the loving union of a man and a woman distinguished not for being particularly charismatic, fashionable, famous or wealthy but for being steadfastly true to themselves. Hubert, Anglo-Italian to his core, was a private and disciplined man. Lelia, born of a half-Italian father and an American mother, and therefore less Italian than Hubert, benefited (as did her fiancé) from a cosmopolitan background but always came across to her family and friends as a private person, shy and even elusive. Like Hubert she could have worn her inherited status on her sleeve. Instead, she was modest, warm-hearted, patient, gentle, exquisitely discreet, and well-mannered.

Hubert with his niece Joan Howard, Ullswater, 1950

Lelia with her parents Roffredo and Marguerite at her wedding
reception, Tetton House, Somerset, 17 September 1951

The marriage celebration took place in England, on 17 September
1951, at St George's Catholic Church in Taunton, Somerset. Roffredo
and Marguerite Caetani came over from Rome and were joined by a wide
circle of Howards. Philip, a nephew, and future Lord Howard of Penrith,
acted as page. The distinguished New Testament scholar, Monsignor
Ronald Knox, preached with his customary eloquence, observing that the
reason the nuptial ring was given to the bride was because women were
so much better at keeping things.[10] A fine reception took place at nearby
Tetton House, home of Hubert's Herbert cousins.[11]

HUBERT AND LELIA were close to their mothers and both, in childhood
and adolescence, had experience of life lived abroad. Much of Lelia's early
education was received, as was Hubert's, from a succession of tutors and
experts, and she also had the benefit of exposure to her mother and father's

rich literary and artistic circle. In any year she might move between Italy, France and Switzerland just as Hubert and his brothers, having been privately tutored in childhood, were subject to the international trajectory of their father's diplomatic career. The result was that Hubert and Lelia, as well as speaking several languages, were immersed in history and culture. The one formative difference between them was that in 1918, as World War I ended, Hubert gained independence from his parents upon being sent to boarding school in England, whereas Lelia may only have enjoyed the fullest sense of her independence after she married Hubert, thirty-three years later. Hubert and Lelia shared with one another the tragedy of having lost a brother. As we recall, Hubert's eldest brother Esmetto had died of illness in 1926, while Lelia's brother Camillo had died in action during Mussolini's invasion of Albania in 1940.

Hubert quickly recognised the degree to which Lelia was immersed in family affairs and how she willingly helped her father in the administration of the estates. Hubert's competence and efficiency reduced the family workload, while for Lelia it also meant having at her side someone who was temperamentally compatible and who understood her personal needs and aspirations. This symbiosis of personal values and perspectives boosted Lelia's confidence, with the result (as many have attested) that her personality was now able to blossom. Adding to their mutual fulfilment was the recovery of Lelia's hitherto dormant Catholic faith, gently rekindled by Hubert.

THE CAETANI, like the Howards, came into prominence in the twelfth century, and both their ducal families have enriched the histories of their respective countries. While their political stock and fortunes may have risen and fallen with the times, both houses produced a succession of outstanding statesmen, soldiers, scholars and patrons of the arts. The families were no less replete with men and women religious – nuns, priests and cardinals, not to mention two Caetani popes and a Howard saint – and, just as Howards had fought at Bosworth Field in 1485 and at Flodden in 1513, Lelia's forebears had taken their place at the Battle of Lepanto in 1571.

Hubert had a strong admiration and affection for the Caetani, and defended the family name as much as he did that of the Howards. On one occasion, a council member of the Roffredo Caetani Foundation wrote and published an historic account of the fifteenth-century Caetani at Sermoneta. In the process he got some of the facts wrong and this greatly upset Hubert. Even before he married, Hubert had immersed himself in Caetani history, a history that marks every step of the Tyrrhenian coastland – from Pisa to Rome, from Cisterna, Ninfa, Sermoneta and Anagni and on down to Fondi, Gaeta and Naples.

Edward Gibbon, the celebrated eighteenth-century English historian, rightly observed in his *History of the Decline and Fall of the Roman Empire* that 'the proudest families are content to lose in the darkness of the Middle Ages the tree of their pedigree'. Gelasio Caetani, in his magisterial history of the Caetani family, *Domus Caietana* (1927), conceded as much: 'It should come as no surprise that tracing the origins of central Italy's important families presents almost insurmountable difficulties.'[12] He stated the probability, however, that Caetani roots went back to the ninth century, specifically to Count Anatolio, first Lord of Gaeta, hence 'Gaetani' or Caetani, whose descendants became dukes. The coastal town of Gaeta, known in the classical ages as *Caieta*, was once a seaside resort for affluent Romans. It lies equidistant between Rome and Naples, and was thus strategically placed from a commercial and military point of view. The Gaetani had spread themselves up and down the coast by the eleventh century.

LELIA'S BRANCH of the derivative Caetani family can be traced reliably to the small cathedral town of Anagni, some sixty miles to the north of Gaeta, and set back in the hills. By the early twelfth century, the family had significant properties in the region and had gained in prominence due to two family-related developments.

The first was that in 1118, Giovanni Gaetani, a Benedictine monk of Monte Cassino, succeeded Paschal II to become Pope Gelasius II. The Holy Roman Emperor Henry V, in power from 1111 to 1125, reacted by installing the antipope, Gregory VIII. Gelasius sought refuge in Gaeta, and retaliated by excommunicating Henry, only to die of pleurisy in Cluny a year later.

The second development, which made a far greater mark on Caetani history, centred on Benedetto Caetani (1235–1303), whose family settled in Anagni. In 1294, succeeding the abdicated and hermitic Saint Celestine V, he was elected pope and took the name Boniface VIII.[13] A competent canon lawyer and patron of the arts, the aristocratic and charismatic Boniface founded the Rome University of La Sapienza and renewed the Vatican Library. His pontificate, however, was mired by constant disputes with King Philip IV of France. Indeed, his provocative bull *Unam Sanctam* (1302), an extreme affirmation of papal supremacy, led to the humiliating circumstances of his arrest in Anagni in September 1303, and the pillaging of his palace by Philip's forces. Outraged and shaken, the elderly Boniface died a month later. Always controversial, he was perhaps the last of the medieval emperor-popes.

In his lifetime, the opportunist Boniface had heightened the power of his family through territorial expansion. Notable was his acquisition of the papal fiefdom of Ninfa and other nearby estates which he then passed to one of his nephews. Ninfa, now of strategic importance, was increasingly fortified – although not enough to save it from being ruthlessly sacked in 1381 against a background of papal wars and intra-familial territorial disputes. A simmering rivalry between the Caetani and Colonna families was followed in 1499 by a drama with potentially crippling consequences: the confiscation of all Caetani properties by the Borgia Pope, Alexander VI. Happily, these were restored by Pope Julius II in 1504, soon after his accession. In spite of this confrontational climate, the Caetani further increased their influence, particularly in the Pontine region. The impregnable Caetani Castle at Sermoneta is an enduring monument to the family's former power, no less than the now-ruined town of Ninfa nearby, with its 100-foot landmark tower, a ducal castle and town

The ruins of the church of Santa Maria Maggiore at Ninfa

hall, seven churches, two convents and many private houses – indeed all the relics of a once-bustling civic, military and religious centre.

After the two Caetani popes Gelasius and Boniface came two six-teenth-century cardinals from the Sermoneta branch of the family: Niccolò, appointed when only fourteen, and his nephew Enrico.[14] Enrico's elder brother Onorato Caetani (1542–92), 5th Duke of Sermoneta, epitomises the family's military prowess and was captain-general of the papal infantry at Lepanto (1571).[15]

In the late seventeenth century, Francesco Caetani (1594–1683), 8th Duke of Sermoneta and Viceroy of Sicily, made efforts to bring life back to wounded and slumbering Ninfa. He used it as an extension of his gardens at nearby Cisterna, mainly to grow flowers. He is particularly remembered for his propagation of tulips, fashionable at the time. The 11th Duke of Sermoneta, another Francesco Caetani (1738–1810), also busied himself with the work of reviving Ninfa, so much so that in 1771 a devoted tenant set a plaque into the wall of the old town hall, giving credit to the duke for 'having raised the waters, built the bridges, restored the mills, repaired the access road, and rebuilt the house and a large granary from their foundations'.[16]

While the Appian Way, following the western flank of the Lepini Mountains and passing through the Pontine estates of the Caetani, was one of the most important military and commercial thoroughfares in Roman and medieval times, the surrounding land was no less prized, as we read from an eighteenth-century manuscript:[17]

> Il territorio si distingue in campi aperti, piani, colli, valli, selve, paludi, e monti, alcuni coltivabili et altri nudi, e vestite di selve... È tutto irrigato dall'acque, che divise in mare, fiumi, stagni, laghi, rivi, e fonti, lo circondano, lo rinfrescano, lo fecondano, et arricchiscono, non solo coll'umore mà anche con abondanza di buoni pesci.

> The land is made up of open fields, plains, hills, valleys, forests, marshland and mountains, parts of which can be cultivated while others are barren or covered by trees... It is well irrigated by waters, being surrounded by sea, rivers, ponds, lakes, coastland and springs, that fertilise and enrich it, not only with well-being but with an abundance of good fish.

This lush Pontine heartland of the Caetani, essentially the Sermoneta estates, had at one time a boundary of 100 miles. From ancient times, though, there was one colossal impediment, namely the Pontine Marshes. These had the effect of periodically making the Appian Way impassable. While the counter-effect was to tighten the trade and military corridors between Rome and Naples and thereby make them commercially exploitable, malaria was persistent and uncompromising.

Successive attempts were made to restore the marshland to what Pliny described as the 'blossoming landscape' that had existed at the time of the Volsci tribal settlers in 500 BC. For centuries, Roman emperors, including Trajan, vainly sought the means; then, with Ninfa a papal possession, popes tried their hand, among them Boniface VIII, in 1298, and Sixtus V, who died of malaria in 1590 after a visit to the marshes. The seventeenth and eighteenth-century Dukes of Sermoneta were likewise unsuccessful.

Only in the twentieth century was the challenge met, and the genius behind it was Lelia's uncle, Gelasio. Cultivated, diplomatic and resourceful like his father Onorato, he was not the kind of person one might associate with explosives. He knew all about them, however, having worked in his early career with several American mining companies, and having used his expertise to devastating effect during Italy's Alpine war with Austria, between 1915 and 1917. The war over, he then turned those same skills to devising a plan for the marshes. The reclamation work, which included the use of explosives to create a series of drainage canals, was carried out

Prince Gelasio Caetani, Lelia's uncle, *c.*1920–*c.*1925

in collaboration with armies of immigrant labour provided by the Italian state. It was officially completed in 1939.

Palaces and strongholds associated with the Caetani remain – in Anagni and Gaeta, of course, but also in Cisterna, Ninfa, Sermoneta and Fondi. Looking back, though, the Caetani story is not just one of power or survival. The last century alone produced several generations of the family steeped in the arts, in music and in scholarship. It is not hard to understand the extent to which the colourful history of the Caetani engrossed Hubert, not only from his perspective as an historian but also as an appeal to his fertile imagination.

FOLLOWING THEIR marriage in 1951, the uppermost apartment of the Palazzo Caetani, most recently occupied by Mondi and Cécile, became Hubert and Lelia's Roman home. It was always bathed in light even though the ceilings were low and the windows small compared with those on the lower floors. On the ample, tiled terrace outside the sitting room was an arrangement of citrus trees in large clay tubs. A small wrought-iron spiral staircase led up to a roof terrace almost the size of a tennis court. From there, on any sunny evening, with thousands of swallows zigzagging in the fading heat, Hubert and Lelia could enjoy a majestic panorama of the city – from the dome of St Peter's Basilica and so many landmark churches standing tall above the terracotta roofs, to the cold, gleaming and incongruous 'Vittoriano', and on to the Forum and the Baths of Caracalla beyond.

Hubert returned to the Tower in early 1952, to catch up with his affairs and to see his relatives. He wrote to Lelia on 24 March, shortly before leaving again to rejoin her. He described 'slight mists in the morning, with great stillness in the air on the water,' and how sad he was not to have her with him 'all these lovely days'. Keenly anticipating his imminent return, he exclaims, 'What great joy, what immense happiness for us to be together again. I shall skip for joy like the lambs in spring at seeing you again. I shall end this letter now sending you my infinite, measureless love.'[18]

Entrance view of the courtyard of Palazzo Caetani in Rome

Hubert's delight at being married to Lelia was accompanied by a strong desire to serve her family, and he never underestimated the weight of Roffredo and Lelia's responsibilities for conserving the Caetani patrimony. Now that he was installed as a member of the family, and with his gifts for administration, the future of the Caetani estates seemed more promising. It was therefore a matter of family sadness that Hubert and Lelia were not blessed with the children they had hoped for.

Lelia gardening at Lyulph's Tower, *c.* 1953

IN THE early 1950s, never for a minute neglecting the garden which she and Lelia tended to in a happy familial collaboration, Marguerite was particularly busy with *Botteghe Oscure*, her increasingly well-known literary review which appeared twice a year.[19] Roffredo, having completed the bulk of his work as a composer before the war, was now in his eighties and battling valiantly to put the Caetani estates onto a productive and secure footing. Increasingly he depended on Hubert's enthusiasm, reliability and sense of good order. This, in turn, took pressure off Marguerite, while Lelia found more time to paint and to prepare for exhibitions.

Although mainly self-taught, Lelia was tutored for a while in Paris by Édouard Vuillard and by Pierre Bonnard, friends of her mother. After the family moved to Italy in 1932, faced with concerns about the family patrimony and the rise of fascism, Lelia's painting sensibilities moved away from the cosmopolitan and more towards nature. At the heart of her artistic expression was Ninfa, which she painted in *tempera* in a highly individualistic style: tonal sensitivity, fine observation, and a delightfully simple and unaffected touch that seemed to mirror her own personality. Her often cloudy but never threatening skies told of her affection for Cumberland where, with Hubert, she took annual summer holidays to avoid the famed *sol leone* of southern Lazio.

It is hard for any writer to convey the magic of Ninfa, but childhood recollections provide some of the truest and most vivid accounts. Benedetta Origo, elder daughter of Iris Origo, who had known Hubert since childhood and was a close friend of the Caetani, went there often:[20]

My sister Donata and I visited Ninfa with our parents on many lovely spring days in the 1950s, when Marguerite and Roffredo invited friends to lunch in the garden. Guests would sit in their pretty linens and hats under the bower overlooking the river, conversation flowing as brilliantly as the clear water below. But we little girls were allowed to picnic in the garden (so much luckier than the grownups!), free to roam at will, as free as the trout which we could sometimes glimpse among the reeds. Our first stop was always the wishing well surrounded by a tall bamboo grove, where we would throw in a pebble for luck. Little canals with freezing waters criss-crossed each other, precarious half-ruined bridges straddled the rushing river below challenging our balance, a sweet medlar tree offered its fruit, roses rose up high on cypress trees, crumbling churches had faded frescoes to discover, paths were bordered with lavender, and the scent of grapefruit stored in the villa cellar were for us the stuff that dreams are made of.

It is beyond the scope of this biography to add to the many tributes, evaluations, scholarly studies and books that have emerged over the years about Marguerite as a prominent patron of the arts: through her active role in Les Amis de l'Art Contemporain in Paris, and her promotion, through her two celebrated review periodicals, of emerging twentieth-century literature.[21] Her literary estate, including the prolific correspondence between her and her many contributors, resides now with the Camillo Caetani Foundation in Rome, founded by Roffredo and Marguerite in 1956, in memory of the son they had lost. Within the estate, the twenty-five volumes of *Botteghe Oscure* (1948–60), when added to her earlier, Paris-based review, *Commerce* (1924–32), are testament to an extraordinary woman with fresh ideas and the energy to go with them. *Botteghe Oscure*, moreover, partially filled the emotional void caused by the wartime death of Camillo, but it was also a significant drain on her personal resources. With Hubert's presence in the family, however, and with the literary and scholarly figure of Giorgio Bassani at Marguerite's side to help assess the streams of literary submissions, it was at last possible to move forward from the uncertainties and tragedies of the war.[22]

As the new Duchess of Sermoneta, and being particularly well known for her accessibility and generosity as a patron, Marguerite found herself at the epicentre of an ever-widening international circle of writers, poets, musicians, artists and intellectuals. Roffredo and Marguerite were engaging hosts and the celebrated Ninfa guestbook reveals not only the variety and distinction of their guests but, by the sheer numbers of them, the extent of their generosity. The Caetani tradition of al fresco lunch parties by the river at Ninfa continued in full flow, enriched from time to time by the presence of statesmen and diplomats, and occasionally of royalty – Elizabeth, the Queen Mother, signed the visitors' book on 21 April 1959. Inevitably, too, the variety of visitors included prominent gardeners and estate owners, some with properties that were grand in scale and lavishly endowed with rare collections of art and artefacts. Ninfa offered little to match such splendour, but the garden's beauty and atmosphere simply defied comparison.

Roffredo Caetani died in the spring of 1961, at a time when Marguerite's memory had begun to diminish. The blow was compounded for Hubert when news came from Hampton Court Palace, early in January 1963, that his ninety-five-year-old mother was fading. By then stooped and petite, Isabella one day complained about feeling giddy, so she was put to bed and soon thereafter lost consciousness. Hubert immediately flew to England to join his brothers at her bedside. Isabella died peacefully on 20 January – a perfect death for one whose innocent faith and transparent goodness must have carried her straight to God, with no purgatorial stops on the way. On 24 January, a bitter day with snow on the ground (it was one of the coldest winters on record), the sons, families and friends came together for her burial in the Howard of Penrith plot at St Philip Howard Cathedral in Arundel, next to her husband Esme and her beloved Esmetto.

Marguerite died in December that same year. Roffredo's work as a composer lives on through the two Caetani foundations, comprising not only a considerable body of musicological interpretation but also the manuscripts and recordings of his piano and chamber music. So too does Marguerite's remarkable contribution to the flowering of early twentieth-century literature find lively and continuing expression in the admirable conferences and academic publications of the Camillo Caetani Foundation.[23]

THE PASSING of Roffredo and Marguerite meant the beginning of an intense new life for Hubert and Lelia, both in relation to one another and to the Caetani properties. The recurring image of the four of them assembled in the *salone* of the villa at Ninfa, like a medieval tableau, each at work in their respective corners – Roffredo perhaps at the piano given to him by his godfather, Franz Liszt (1811–86); Marguerite reading a manuscript for *Botteghe Oscure*; Hubert poring over the estate budgets; and Lelia painting by one of the two north-facing windows – was now a memory. Considerable emotional adjustment was needed.

Hubert and Lelia were soothed by the peace and solitude of Ninfa, and their understanding of it is extraordinarily well captured in a poem by Elizabeth Jennings, written after a visit to the garden in April 1958. In it, Jennings picks up from Hubert that his and Lelia's work there was one of stewardship, not only of the Caetani patrimony but also, as Hubert must have expressed it, of the 'engrafted word of God' as invoked in verse three.

One can only imagine the conversation as Hubert and Lelia led Jennings out past the arboreta, to the fields where 'corn and nut-trees grew':[24]

> I never cared for such an ordered view.
> Blenheim, Stowe, Versailles were worth no more
> Than afternoons of just an hour or two.
> I've always wanted wildness in the sky,
> A Turner tempest and a garden where
> The roses grew the way they wished. The eye
>
> Found its own patterns. Two hours out of Rome
> A garden grew in Ninfa. High above,
> Norma was pitched. This was a prince's home
> And I was greeted with a welcome which
> Takes centuries to turn into a love
> Part courtesy and part a shared and rich
>
> Yet economic luxury. A man
> Of an old English family who had
> Married the prince's daughter showed me land
> Where corn and nut-trees grew. Showing the last
> He spoke of 'The engrafted word of God'
> And suddenly I saw the careful past
>
> Of a long line of owners who also
> Were stewards who must tend but not possess.
> Where gardens are allowed much space to grow
> And cared for quietly I've slowly come
> To understand there is most happiness.

Much, rightly, has been written about Lelia's imprint on Ninfa as a romantic garden, where the roses 'grew the way they wished'. She certainly made fundamental changes to the planting and visual aspects of the Ninfa she had inherited from her mother. She was open to experiment, as the seasons were far from predictable other than in their sequence. Many plants had to be replaced or switched around. Hubert was a willing novice, and began the first ever attempt to catalogue the plant collection and, with Lelia, to order from their many suppliers in Italy and abroad. They rejoiced in the rock garden or *colletto*, covering the site of a collapsed medieval wall and watchtower; it became a focus of their personal attention because of its potential for colour and diversity. There they spent quiet evenings together, weeding, planting and planning its development. They loved and respected the garden and the estate workers, and their families. Often, they would visit their homes together and share their meals.

It is notable that Hubert and Lelia's years together at Ninfa became gradually far less centred on socialising in the old way, with the result that they were able to turn their attention increasingly to their close friends and family in England, many of whom had been given the unforgettable experience of staying at magical Ninfa or at the Caetani Castle at Sermoneta. Hubert and Lelia's recuperative summer visits to Lyulph's Tower were also the catalyst for family gatherings, or for walks or games in the lakeside meadows where Hubert had once grazed his cows. Their journeys to and from England were mostly by car so that they could spend time together walking in Switzerland, well known to Hubert from childhood and from the last, sad days of his brother Esmetto.

Owing, no doubt, to his upbringing as a diplomat's son, Hubert presented himself as rather formal – certainly in Rome, where for the most part he preferred to wear a suit and tie, never a blazer. The idea of 'smart casual' would have seemed to him a contradiction in terms. He could be groomed like an ambassador on the most formal occasions, such as meeting a pope or a head of state. At Ninfa, by contrast, he was often to be seen walking about in a cardigan and tie; while in summer, he would occasionally put on a voluminous pair of khaki shorts and a floppy white sun hat. Occasionally, when the heat was hardly bearable, he would plunge into the icy river. Lelia, for the most part, favoured a matching jacket and skirt, and, because she was as tall as Hubert, flat shoes. She always came across as understatedly elegant, and, with her father's facial features and her almost invariably netted hair, was striking to look at. She was gentle and withdrawn by nature, and at the same time touchingly responsive to the fervent loyalty of those who worked on the Caetani estates. In England, Lelia preferred to be known simply as 'Mrs Howard'.

When, in 1974, she and Hubert moved from the main villa at Ninfa during necessary restoration works, and took up residence across the river at the Foresteria (originally a medieval rectory and later home to a family of estate workers), they did so with unconcealed delight. They brought in the simplest of furnishings and surrounded themselves with books. Neither knew how to cook, and so there always had to be someone available to prepare their meals. Even after works on their main house had been completed, they stayed on there for a while, preferring the greater peace and solitude that it afforded. Needless to say, the villa itself was redecorated to a high standard – but one of elegant simplicity and faultless taste.

Perceptions of the Caetani family in the Pontine region, notwithstanding their traditional generosity and great enterprise over the centuries, were sometimes tinged with an almost feudal suspicion. This attitude undoubtedly gained traction as the fascists, the new so-called heroes of the ordinary people, took control of Italy in the 1930s.

In his biographical work *Il Vassallo della Musica*, Riccardo Cerocchi (architect, music lover and former chair of the Roffredo Caetani Foundation) touchingly reveals something of this tension. In a chapter entitled 'L'invito Inaspettato' ('The Unexpected Invitation'), he recounts how, in the autumn of 1973, he and his wife Maria Teresa received a formal written invitation to join Hubert and Lelia for lunch at Ninfa. They had not met before and we find Cerocchi consumed with curiosity, unable to imagine why he, with 'no particular distinction except that of working hard for his family's very existence', had been chosen.

Admitting, humbly, to an inferiority complex gained from his student days in Rome, where he had encountered the sons and daughters of the capital's rich and noble families as they arrived in fancy cars at the School of Architecture, but encouraged by his wife Maria Teresa's realism and her fearless 'apostolic vision as a fervent advocate of Catholic Action', [25]he prepares himself to meet Hubert and Lelia. On arrival at Ninfa, what were to be the appropriate protocols? Does he kiss Lelia's hand, give her a bunch of flowers, make a short speech? Instead, as he put it, 'the meeting was as natural as is possible', and 'in their inimitable way' the 'Signori' put them completely at their ease, being 'wonderful human beings and not at all different from others'.

It was a seminal encounter. Not only was it the start of a friendship, but also the moment when Hubert and Lelia were able to plan with them both a fruitful association between the Roffredo Caetani Foundation (part of whose aim is the diffusion of Roffredo Caetani's musical works, and the development of Hubert and Lelia's nascent chamber-music festival at Sermoneta) and the growing International Music Campus, which Cerocchi founded in 1970. Much later, in 1978, Cerocchi would be invited to join the council of the foundation, and on Hubert's death, in 1987, succeeded him as chairman.[26]

THE RELATIONSHIP between Hubert and Lelia was touching to all who knew them. They shared a rhythm of life that, although seemingly unhurried as it was not in their nature to rush, brings to mind words from an Italian proverb: 'Chi va piano va lontano' ('He who goes slowly goes far'). The temperamental differences remained, Lelia's calm nature counterbalancing Hubert's well-known tendency to worry and to be at times fussy and indeed censorious. One of Hubert's great-nephews, Dominic Howard, includes this passage among his fond memories of them both:

> I remember as a boy walking with Hubert on a hot day in July in the hills above Ninfa. We were both wearing shorts, his being a pair of 'khaki empire-builders'. On his head sat a floppy white hat. The path narrowed to a point where it was thick with nettles. Without a word he put me on his back and, uncomplaining, walked on ... There was only one occasion on which he was displeased with me – at least one in which he openly showed his displeasure. On a beautiful summer's

Lelia at Lyulph's Tower, 1973

day at the Tower, when I was aged nine or ten, I grabbed a fluffy white towel from Hubert and Lelia's bathroom and ran to Aira Force to swim in the pool at the bottom of the waterfall. I ran back, got changed and put a now rather muddy towel back in their bathroom. When Hubert discovered this crime, he asked me, in an agitated voice, to apologise to Lelia. The walk from my bedroom, down the corridor and up the steps into the sitting room, felt about a mile long. Lelia was waiting for me in a wing chair, a benign smile on her face. Even before I had opened my mouth, I knew I'd been forgiven.[27]

Lelia was indeed a patient and unflappable person. On one occasion at Ninfa, after some small altercation, a hot-headed cook lost his temper with her and swung a punch, missing her jaw by a hair's breadth. With great dignity, she rebuked him with the words, 'Don't be so silly.' The man, suitably chastened, returned to the kitchen as if nothing had happened. Only once was Lelia known in the family to have uttered a deprecation, very mild and very suitable, that came during a frenetic and highly competitive card game at Ninfa – Racing Demon.

Hubert and Lelia, like so many couples, delighted in humorous badinage, and no meal with them was ever dull as Hubert had a wealth of stories to tell and delighted in conversation. His way of laughing was in discreet, soft-voiced interjections rather than in torrential bursts, while Lelia's humour, reserved when they first married, increasingly adapted to his. Like many good raconteurs, Hubert was apt to embellish his recollections here and there, often drawing his occasionally fanciful but always well-observed humour from the time-consuming vagaries of Italian bureaucracy, of which he despaired at times, or the dark history of the Tudor and Elizabethan Howards. Giacomo Antonelli never forgot how Hubert, at Ninfa, took to wearing very frayed shirts as a means of economising. Gently admonished by Lelia, Hubert explained that this was how country gentlemen dressed in England, to which Lelia retorted, 'But you are overdoing it.'[28]

HUBERT AND LELIA'S twenty-five-year marriage created a bond between two remarkable families and in the process enriched both. There is a certain symbolism in the story that, after the death of his mother, Hubert retrieved from her high-ceilinged apartment at Hampton Court the tapestry of the Howard coat of arms that had been woven to honour his father's elevation to the peerage in 1930. In view of its size, not even the Tower was suitable for it, so with Lelia's permission he transferred it to the Casa del Cardinale (part of the Caetani Castle at Sermoneta), whose interior walls are of ample height. There it hung on two nails for half a century, its delicate fabric and needlework unprotected from winter damp. Then, in 2016, the Roffredo Caetani Foundation took the welcome initiative of arranging to have it restored by experts in Rome. It is now back in its original position, framed and behind glass; an enduring sign of the brief but fruitful Howard presence within the history of Lelia's family.

IN EARLY 1971, Lelia began suffering from a mild heart condition and Hubert, unable to find a solution in Italy, brought her to London where she had a successful operation. Life resumed, now under the menacing shadow of the terrorist Red Brigades who, for the rest of the decade, were to affect the life and political climate of Italy.[29] This, and the endless conservational challenges facing Hubert every day, were not as disheartening as the dreadful news, which came in autumn 1976, that Lelia was seriously ill with cancer. The reputable London Clinic did its best for her but to no avail. Before Christmas, the author drove Hubert and Lelia to the village of Castle Hedingham in Essex where she spent her last days in the care of their old friend, the Queen's doctor and homeopath, Margery Blackie. She died peacefully on 11 January 1977, with Hubert and a small group of family members at her side.

No one expected, with the loss of Lelia, that Ninfa could ever be quite the same again.

CHAPTER EIGHT

A Conservationist at Heart

A n inevitable concern for Roffredo and Marguerite Caetani was the destiny of the family patrimony, following the tragic loss of their son Camillo. Roffredo had successfully petitioned his old friend King Victor Emmanuel III, the last Italian monarch, to allow the patrimony to pass through the female line, ensuring that Lelia would be able, as her parents wished, to inherit and thus to carry on her work at Ninfa, conserving the garden, and to an extent reimagining it through her artistic vision. The issue, however, ran far deeper; something Hubert fully understood. After the war, historic estates and monuments in private hands were becoming increasingly burdensome to maintain. When Roffredo sought his advice, Hubert was able to speak knowledgeably not only about the work of the well-established National Trust in Britain (at the time responsible for conserving up to a quarter of the Lake District National Park), but also about the role of foundations as tax-exempt, non-profit-making entities. He had, after all, worked for the Carnegie Foundation.

Two developments of the 1950s, attributable significantly to Hubert's influence, were the creation of Italia Nostra in 1955 and the Camillo Caetani Foundation in 1956. Italia Nostra based itself on the founding principle of the National Trust, established in England in 1895, which is that people need historic, beautiful and natural places for their identity and their pleasure. Hubert and a number of his like-minded friends felt passionately that Italy could benefit from something similar. To that purpose, on 29 October 1955, they gathered together in the Rome offices of a notary at 18, Via degli Uffici del Vicario, to frame a constitution for Italia Nostra, whose most urgent focus was to oppose – successfully as it turned out – the demolition of parts of Rome's historic centre. Among those founders present with Hubert were Umberto Zanotti Bianco, Giorgio Bassani, Desideria Pasolini dall'Onda and Elena Croce.[1]

The constitutional Act itself, written in the spidery handwriting of a public official and bearing a 200 lire stamp, was based on this unequivocal premise:

> That those present, like all who care about the artistic and natural beauties of our country and cannot fail to be extremely worried about the increasingly serious and intense process of destruction to which our national heritage has been subjected in recent years, have therefore decided to set up a National Foundation with the aim of arousing a more lively interest in the problems inherent in the conservation of the countryside, of the monuments and of the environmental character of the cities, especially in relation to the development of modern urban planning.[2]

In Article 3, the example of the National Trust is specifically cited. The scope of the new association was wide, and over the course of time Italia Nostra would spread its wings and create links with other, similar organisations. On Hubert's initiative a Latina branch was opened in 1957, of which he became the first chairman. Such were Hubert's sustained efforts over the years that much later, in 1982, Italia Nostra awarded him the prestigious Zanotti Bianco prize for his 'exemplary' work in the preservation of Italy's cultural heritage.

The first meeting of the Rome-based Camillo Caetani Foundation, registered on 10 May 1956, was a critical step in securing a lasting solution to the diverse conservational problems posed by the family patrimony, consisting principally of the sixteenth-century Palazzo Caetani in Via delle Botteghe Oscure, and the country estates of Ninfa and Sermoneta.

The palazzo seemed to be the obvious place to start. The first meeting, with Lelia in the chair as foundress and Hubert the architect of the process, was propitious. Giacomo Antonelli, the foundation's lawyer, would later recall Hubert's close attention to the selection of the first councillors, among them representatives of the State Archive, the Fine Arts Academy, and the Vatican Museum.

The Caetani archive is a treasury of family records dating from medieval times, of materials concerning Italy's early history, specifically the history of Rome, and of the papacy and the Papal States (we recall the two Caetani popes). At that time, it already included a rare library, various papal bulls and codices, and the growing literary estate of Lelia's mother. All of these needed cataloguing so that over time, according to the foundation's outgoing remit, they could be made available to researchers, writers and scholars. As the work of the foundation gathered pace, the scale and complexity of its undertaking became clear and, in 1974, the council invited the distinguished Vatican librarian and archivist, Luigi Fiorani, to oversee the work on a part-time basis. This he did, with dedication, until his untimely death in 2009. Soon thereafter, in a happy continuity, his daughter Caterina took charge of the archive, having understudied him there for a number of years.

Hubert, who had foreseen perfectly how post-war Italy would need to focus on the material and the modern, was now embarked on something of a crusade. In this regard, the two foundations provided him with perfect platforms and a role which suited him extremely well, and which he would probably never have imagined. As an historian he would make it his business to conserve and bring order to the archival treasures in Palazzo Caetani; as a passionate environmentalist, he would focus on Ninfa and the Pontine region. The author, historian and garden expert Charles Quest-Ritson, who has written often about Ninfa, sums up Hubert's mindset as follows:

Even before World War II he had actively promoted a more wholesome view of the world and how its resources should be managed. At Ninfa, he argued for a greater commitment to environmental principles – including the limited use of artificial fertilizers, the eschewal of herbicides and restraint with insecticides...More importantly he foresaw the degradation of the whole environment that would accompany Italy's post-war economic recovery and the popular expectation of rising standards of living.[3]

THERE IS no doubt that, within a few years of taking his place in the bosom of the Caetani family, Hubert became a persuasive ambassador for conservation, participating in a busy schedule of meetings and conferences at which he took every opportunity to appeal to those in authority to adopt measures for environmental protection. He was soon known to members of central and local government: to senators, prefects, mayors, and to planning authorities. He made friends with the heads of Italy's most important national parks, as well as estate owners and farmers in the area around Ninfa.

The boast that Mussolini had once made to Hubert's father, about his push towards agricultural expansion in the 1930s, seemed momentarily fulfilled in the Pontine region, when the Caetani family's significant share of the marshes was drained by the fascists and then converted into a lush patchwork of fields and plantations. Economic injustice there may have been, in that most of the family's land in the so-called Agro Pontino (at one time consisting of 200,000 acres) was subsequently sequestered by the fascists. However, in the two decades after the war, those many visitors who stood on the battlements of the Caetani Castle and looked south along the Tyrrhenian coastline towards Monte Circeo, could marvel at the spectacle and the peacefulness of this fertile countryside. It was a sensation heightened towards dusk when silvery arcs of water would begin criss-crossing the landscape and working their magic on the crops. Sadly, perhaps inevitably, all such harmony would soon begin to dissipate as the battles for the environment began.

One such was the battle for the hillsides close to Ninfa, which began not long after Hubert's marriage to Lelia. By the late 1940s, with cement now one of the most sought-after ingredients for the urban regeneration of Italy, the limestone Lepini hills had become a magnet for developers. To the north, south and east of Ninfa, they gouged away: first the steep northern flank of the hill on which Sermoneta stands, then the beautiful slopes covered with olive trees directly behind Ninfa, where a quarry company began operations in 1954. Lime quarrying involves not just the sound of intermittent blasting, but it results in clouds of dust which settle on plants and vegetation, preventing photosynthesis. At this time, and with no recourse to the law since none then existed for the purpose, Lelia made the choice of acquiring the site notwithstanding the extortionate price demanded. She managed this by selling a parcel of farmland. Her ingenious planting of the gaping wound left by the quarriers minimised the visual impact for future generations.

Hubert and Lelia moved now to pressure the authorities into ring-fencing some of the territory around Ninfa in order to create an environmental and monumental protection area, free from poaching and shooting. This process, with all its twists and turns, took until 1959. The outlook appeared to brighten. In 1963, however, on a day when Hubert was walking his dog Orsetta among the olive groves on the slopes behind Ninfa, slightly north of the earlier quarry, he chanced upon a number of red marker posts sticking out of the ground. He asked a shepherd what they were and discovered that Italcementi, Italy's largest cement producer, was due to start limestone quarrying there within a few weeks. A contract had already been drawn up with the local authorities of Norma on the hilltop above. Hubert rushed back to his office and began a series of calls to friends in government. The son of Italcementi's chairman was eventually persuaded to travel down from Bergamo. He took one look at the garden and realised immediately that if the project were to go ahead Ninfa would be dead within months. The contract was cancelled. A few furious inhabitants of Norma parked a loudspeaker van on the other side of the lake and broadcast hostile messages to Hubert and Lelia for several days, accusing them of blocking progress and destroying jobs.

Close to the monastery at Valvisciolo, a mile to the south of Ninfa, work soon began on another quarry – illegal, as it turned out, but on a far greater scale. Without adequate laws in place, Hubert was unable to oppose this during his lifetime. When the law finally caught up with the operators, it was too late. The abandoned site still stands today – a purposeless disfigurement of the hillside. To make matters worse the local authorities have still not removed the jutting structures and concrete loading bays clearly visible from the foot of the hill.

Neither Hubert nor Lelia opposed progress, but both believed in control and good practice within conservational laws that needed constant revision and enforcement. The laws may be better understood and applied these days, but in those post-war decades, the race towards modernity and expansion began to leave its ugly traces all over the Pontine country-side. Cement, the product of quarrying, is vital, of course, and it was rightly used to improve road and railway infrastructure throughout Italy, although today the maintenance of the highways up and down the Pontine coast is woefully underfunded. In terms of commercial and residential building, the early 1950s heralded a rush to construct private houses and apartment blocks in the area, many unregulated and hideous, some the product of speculation.

THE YEAR 1970 was declared 'A Year for Nature' by the Italian authorities, an important milestone which brought optimism to the environmentalists of Italy. On 9 May, Hubert, ever the missionary when it came to worth-while causes, made a keynote speech at a conference held in Latina, entitled 'Per la Natura'. In it he differentiated quite pointedly between '*l'uomo tecnico*' – loosely 'technical man' – and '*l'uomo sapiens*', the first of whom seeks limited profit-making objectives without taking account of the wider and ruinous consequences of his actions, the second of whom treads with wisdom, caution and measure. To explain *l'uomo tecnico*, Hubert used the example of the insecticide DDT and its misleadingly successful use as an anti-malarial disinfectant, not just in the Pontine marshland area following the reclamation, but widely and in many countries. He asked, incredulously, how DDT, with its damaging impact on human health, on

Hubert walking in the hills above Ninfa, *c.* 1977

wildlife and on the environment, could have escaped regulation for so long. And how, in the Pontine Region, as in the whole of Italy, huge numbers of weekend *cacciatori* (shooting parties) were still able to roam the hills, woods and pastures randomly shooting some of the rarest birds in the natural cycle, and disturbing the rural peace. Hubert's speech, infused with technical knowledge derived from his practical experience of nature and farming methods, concluded with one of his passionate, though deeply pragmatic, appeals. It was addressed, first, to the provincial authorities and conservation societies, urging them to bring about change, to take up the cause at every level, and to create parklands, protected areas, forests and other habitats for flora and fauna. Second, to industry, urging it to confine its expansion to areas less well suited to natural conservation, and to take its share of responsibility for the environment. With great foresight (because so many of his ideas were eventually acted upon), Hubert urged nothing less than a national debate: in effect a new charter for conservation in Italy.[4]

Notwithstanding Hubert's lofty vision, widely publicised and increasingly adopted in the Pontine region, this was in reality just the beginning of Italy's post-war environmental movement. Hubert's efforts as a dogged ambassador for Ninfa, which with Lelia he had managed to turn into a much-admired paradigm of good environmental practice, redoubled. Like Lelia, he also had a strong visual sense. In summer 1979, two years after her death, we find him giving a slide-illustrated talk about Ninfa and Sermoneta on Insel Mainau, the German garden-island on Lake Constance, a reputable 'dream garden' designed with the tourist very much in mind. There were at least 250 people present, including Hubert's kinsman George Howard, who had been invited to speak about his family's grandiose property Castle Howard in Yorkshire. Some months later, Hubert wrote to Francis expressing hope that his talk had been acceptable, but observing that the famed Insel Mainau was 'far from what he and Lelia would consider to be a garden at all':

> There is nothing quite like it, because if Coney Island and Blackpool are human ingenuity and creativeness gone crazy, Insel Mainau, alas, is God's nature and His creativeness turned into a caricature by man. Yet two million people visit it and pay four marks; so, with eight million marks each year, or one million pounds, Count Lennart Bernadotte can indulge any floral absurdity and extravagance. The first thing one meets as one enters are enormous peacocks, pheasants and duck made up of petunias, begonias and dahlias.[5]

On his return from Germany, Hubert hosted an Italia Nostra event at Palazzo Caetani, sponsored by the Camillo Caetani Foundation. This was the launching of reprints of Volumes V and VI of Giuseppe and Francesco Tomassetti's seminal work *La Campagna Romana Antica, Medioevale e Moderna.*[6] By way of illustrating Hubert's passion for the environment, few texts compare to his introduction to the proceedings. It invokes not only his perception of the grave and continuing risks to the Roman countryside but also his keen and almost childlike anticipation and sense of escape when, at the end of a busy week in stifling Rome, he would pack up his Chrysler estate car, the rear load covered with a reddish rubberised sheet, inch his way cautiously through the palazzo's narrow *portone* into busy Via delle Botteghe Oscure, and head out past the Caracalla Baths to the open countryside and Ninfa:

> Not long ago, it was still possible to get on a horse at Porta Santo Stefano or Porta del Popolo and quickly, and unhindered, find oneself immersed in the vast and beautiful sweep of the Campagna Romana. Scattered here and there rose the fortified towers of history and legend, and along the route lay an infinite number of ruins and relics of ancient civilisations … The cultural imagination of Europe lit up at the contemplation of so much history and beauty, drawing writers and poets, men of culture and the finest artists, from all centuries and from every country, to nourish themselves from the inexhaustible font of this inspiration.

And then came words of frustration and despair:

> Today, who can still hear a nightingale singing in a sacred space, her song not eclipsed by the sound of motor engines and transistor radios? Who can still enjoy the natural landscape, or observe the variety and splendour of historic monuments through the acrylic colours of posters and advertisements and entanglements of electric wire? The Botticelli-like spring flowers are dead among the ruins, destroyed by the curse of herbicides. Our new barbarity, savage and materialistic, has no desire to embrace a vision, or a reality other than what has already been conditioned by its lowly purposes.[7]

THE RUINED town of Ninfa, with its medieval fortifications and dramatic history, was cherished by Hubert the historian, as was the spectacular early thirteenth-century Caetani Castle at Sermoneta perched on a hilltop, less than five miles away. This formidable redoubt is impregnated with the family's history and still dominates the countryside around Ninfa.

The approach to the main gate of the Caetani Castle at Sermoneta

It was built originally for the Annibaldi family, but was bought from them by the Caetani in 1297. During the papal wars of the fourteenth century, the Caetani of Ninfa and those of Sermoneta became bitterly divided. This led to the brutal sacking of Ninfa in 1381. While Ninfa now lay in ruins on the plain, the victorious family members up on the hill added to the fortifications of their castle. Just over a century later, however, the Borgia Pope, Alexander VI, impulsively excommunicated the Caetani and confiscated all their lands and properties. This state of affairs was short-lived. Soon after Alexander's death in 1503, his successor Julius II restored everything to the aggrieved family. Caetani prestige grew once more, and in 1536 the Holy Roman Emperor Charles V was a guest at the castle.[8] Not wishing to be outdone by his host Boniface Caetani (c.1514–74), 4th Duke of Sermoneta, he arrived with an absurdly large escort of 1,000 knights and 4,000 infantrymen. While Onorato Caetani's heroics at Lepanto some seventy years later again covered the family in glory, by degrees thereafter the great fortress fell into decline, suffering looting in the eighteenth century by French and Spanish troops and having no further military purpose.

At the end of the nineteenth century, the Caetani reoccupied the castle once more and began major works of restoration. These gathered momentum during the lifetime of Gelasio Caetani, Lelia's uncle, but his death in 1934 halted progress. During World War II, which once more interrupted restoration, Marguerite Caetani, and members of her family and some of the estate workers, were obliged to move into the building while the Germans occupied Ninfa, and this also gave them shelter from intensive Allied bombing in the area just prior to the liberation of Rome.

After his marriage to Lelia in 1951, Hubert pondered the state of the castle. Slowly, as money would allow, he set in motion a range of restoration initiatives under the supervision of regional authorities and experts. The scale of the work required was daunting but, over successive decades, the castle was restored to the point where it is now not only a fine tourist attraction but also a beacon of culture and hospitality, offering dramatic space as a museum, a film set and a lively and atmospheric venue for concerts, courses and conferences. The Dukes of Sermoneta, the last of them Lelia's father Roffredo, would surely be united in their relief that the castle is cared for by a foundation dedicated to its restoration and conservation; they would also be delighted that the little town of Sermoneta, clustered around it, is still one of the loveliest in the entire Lepini range.

On 14 April 1981, the Lazio Section of the incipient Associazione Dimore Storiche Italiane, an association for the conservation of Italy's historic homes, held a conference in Latina entitled 'The Foundation, Instrument of Conservation'. It was always said of Hubert that he became the flag bearer in Italy for the National Trust, whose work had so inspired the Caetani foundations. One of just three speakers at this conference, Hubert revisited this theme with characteristic passion, pausing towards the end for a brief slide show to demonstrate to his audience what might be lost to Europe if Ninfa and Sermoneta were not now in the care of a foundation. He spoke with lyrical intensity about the garden, quoting Augustus Hare's *Walks in Rome* in which Hare describes how Ninfa's beauty and peace absorb all the senses.[9] He lamented the Italian state-minded and heavy-handed tendency towards expropriation as a means of resolving issues to do with patrimony. He called for more subtle and differentiated approaches to conservation, reminding his audience of how, in England, successive governments had adopted a system in which, by way of subsidy, it was possible to reduce taxation on historic properties and, as appropriate, keep the owner-managers in place. And he called once more on local authorities and state entities to desist from expropriation, describing the foundation as an ideal *via media* between state and private ownership. Bearing in mind that the Roffredo Caetani Foundation had been created as a private entity to manage a private patrimony, his words that day had a particular resonance.[10]

CHAPTER NINE

The Final Years

'All in this world eventually comes to an end and I thank God for a full and happy life.'

HUBERT HOWARD, *in one of his last letters to a friend*

HUBERT'S desolation at the loss of his precious Lelia in January 1977 is conveyed in a heartfelt and deeply melancholic passage from a letter, dated 12 February 1977, to his brother Mondi soon after her death. It has been quoted often. What makes the passage so poignant is the association Hubert so naturally makes between Lelia, Ninfa, and a world without her. The garden, flowering magnificently even in early February, is depicted as sad and vulnerable, just as Hubert himself was feeling:

Yesterday was the 11th of February [1977], one month exactly since the death of my darling Lelia. I went down to Ninfa, because in the evening there was a service in our local church at Tor Tre Ponti. The garden was so beautiful, full of flowers and blossom, all the magnolias were out, and the prunus, the mimosa, the early daffodils, the wild violets and primulas and so much else besides. Now I walk around alone; and who will care for all those plants? Some seem to have wanted to die with her – the exuberant sweet-smelling *Luculia* which scents the garden around Christmas and lives in a special bamboo hut to protect it from frosts. Up to this year it has flowered every single year of our married life, but perhaps the too-heavy rains have killed it for it is dead. Also, a beautiful *Malus*, which Lelia planted about five years ago, is dying of cancer of the roots … It will be so difficult to wander in this world, which without Lelia has become an underworld. Our journeys through Italy, France and England were such a joy to us and we would always go back or want to go back to the beautiful places we saw together so that she could sketch some more. But when I pick up a postcard of Autun, or a picture of Venice painted by Lelia, I wonder now how I shall be able to see these places again without her. Wherever I have seen her and see her no more, there is an emptiness which is difficult to bear and sometimes almost a meaninglessness in life. However, I know I must combat this feeling and, as long as I have life, be grateful for the gift of living and count my days in patience until, by God's mercy, we can be brought together again.

A few days later, he replied to a supportive message from his younger brother Henry:

The tributes I get about Lelia are so many and also so beautiful. Each one opens up my wound and not a day passes that I do not shed tears. And yet I would not have it otherwise. She was such a wonderful person and we were so happy together that everything around us seemed touched by a Divine Grace and the world was a sort of paradise. Now that death has come to her the divide between life and death seems so much less to me and death is not an unnatural or unnecessary thing to us.[1]

Fortunately, Hubert was accustomed to solitude and so overcame his desolation not so much by leaning on friends and family but by redoubling his responsibilities and immersing himself in his works of conservation. His strength and composure were, as ever, made possible by the intensity of his faith and his love of Lelia. As was his lifelong habit, he attended Mass as often as he could and at Easter would never miss the Triduum. In England, from time to time, he would go on a monastic retreat with his brother Mondi, a nephew or a great-nephew. He prayed often. In this period of emotional frailty, he kept himself as it were tolerably suspended between this world and the next. One could sense that Hubert envisaged that next world as being another Ninfa, a place of complete harmony and reconciliation.

HUBERT PICKED up on his commitments in Rome and at Ninfa with little delay. On 25 November 1978, after considerable preliminary work and planning, he convened a landmark meeting of the general council of the Roffredo Caetani Foundation. Why 'landmark'? The reason was that the foundation, although registered in 1972 with a statute and a rudimentary structure, could not fully function during Lelia's lifetime since she personally needed to retain some of the properties for her own use. The moment had now come for these to be transferred to the foundation, and for the provisions of Lelia's will, published in March 1977, to be accepted in full, including Hubert's entitlement to live as a tenant at both Palazzo Caetani and Ninfa for the rest of his life. (It is interesting to recall that Lelia had wanted to leave Hubert some land, in recognition of his defining role in the establishment of the foundations, and his years of service to her family. This offer, characteristically, he refused.)

The meeting took place at Ninfa, in what was in effect the family's sitting room or *salone*, the old assembly room of the original town hall. Hubert was appointed chair in succession to Lelia, and the first councillors, for the most part nominated by Lelia, were re-elected or appointed. Among them, as vice-chairmen, were Giacomo Antonelli and Riccardo Cerocchi.[2] Crucially, representatives of wildlife and environmental associations, and of leading wildlife parks in Italy, were also invited – including Bonaldo Stringher, a co-founder with Hubert of Italia Nostra in 1955, and Fulco Pratesi and Arturo Osio, respectively vice chairman and managing director of the World Wildlife Fund (WWF). Also appointed that day were the architects Paolo Mora and his wife Laura, of the Central Institute for Restoration in Rome. Of the twenty-three councillors formally signed in at the meeting, nine were invited onto the foundation's steering committee.[3]

The first general secretary to be appointed to the foundation was Lauro Marchetti, whose father had served the Caetani estate with great success since his recruitment just after the war. Lauro, for whom Hubert and Lelia felt an almost parental affection, instinctively loved nature and wildlife, and, as he grew into adolescence, they saw him as being able one day to work for the foundation and possibly curate the garden. From an early age, he had learnt from Hubert the basics of administration and from Lelia her planting methods and unique vision for the garden. He also helped them both with secretarial work.

On 1 November 1979, with an accountancy qualification under his belt, Lauro was officially taken on by the foundation. He became an increasingly valued contributor to many aspects of its work, sharing with Hubert the distinctly old-fashioned and frugal facilities in the office, laboriously handwriting the minutes of the foundation meetings, helping Hubert fight his continuing battles for the environment, and keeping him company on plant-sourcing trips to England. From time to time, Lauro used to drive Hubert about – an experience best forgotten as Hubert was not an easy passenger.

Few in the post-Hubert period can have matched Lauro's accumulated and intimate knowledge of Ninfa's flora and fauna, which he dispensed to visitors with charm and infectious enthusiasm. And so, after Hubert's untimely death less than a decade after that critical 1978 meeting, Lauro Marchetti, as willed by Lelia, began combining his role as the foundation's general secretary with the more conspicuous responsibility of managing the garden. While this provided all the advantages of continuity, the challenge was immense.

Hubert always recognized his good fortune in having so many fine and expert colleagues on the councils of Lelia's foundations, both of which he now chaired. Understandable deference on the part of the councillors and those others who worked for the foundations, however, required him to be at the centre of almost everything. In November 1979, he wrote to his brother Francis describing in these words what his life had become:

a stately dance, a Pavane, where with measured steps I move from one position to another … and with so much to deal with … memoranda, accounts, oppositions, illegalities, surprises and frustrations that beset one like the obscenities of Hieronymus Bosch – but fortunately not of course inside the Council meetings, where we are all friends, but pressing in upon us from the outside, through kinks and keyholes.[4]

ON 19 NOVEMBER 1979, two days after Hubert had introduced and hosted at Palazzo Caetani an important conference on the rare and precious Caetani Dante Codex,[5] another meeting of the foundation's general council meeting took place at Ninfa, to tackle an agenda that typified the breadth and complexity of the challenges facing the Ninfa estate. It was reported that the garden's public visitor numbers that year had risen to nearly 18,000, but that the entry contributions had been insufficient to cover the growing cost of maintaining the garden. Set against this was another bumper year for the California 'gold' peaches, introduced to Ninfa by Gelasio Caetani in the early 1930s, some years after his time as Italian Ambassador to Washington. Nevertheless, this quite fragile state of the foundation's economic affairs resulted in the council members agreeing to raise the garden entrance fees slightly, before moving to another perennial concern, namely the sufficiency of Ninfa's spring waters to meet public consumption as well as the needs of the garden. Hubert, ever the conservationist, reminded the meeting that at the time of the reclamation of the Pontine Marshes all the water to Latina came via aqueducts whereas the local authorities, not for the first time, were now proposing the creation of boreholes, which alarmed Hubert because of their potential to damage the water basin on which Ninfa's springs had relied for so many centuries. The danger was duly averted.

Another concern raised that day by Hubert was the need to expand the existing environmental protection area around the 'oasis of Ninfa', which, with much effort on Hubert and Lelia's part, had been secured in 1957. To that end, Hubert now requested the drawing up of plans to persuade the local authorities to add land surrounding the historic abbey of Valvisciolo, nearby Monte Corvino, and the woodlands between Sermoneta and neighbouring Bassiano. Once more, his initiative was to prove successful.

IN SPITE OF his many duties and obligations to the Caetani foundations in the capital and at Ninfa, Hubert found time for so much more. Always mindful of Lelia's work as an artist, in September 1980 he arranged for thirty-seven of her Cumbrian and Scottish landscapes to be exhibited for a month at the Abbot Hall Art Gallery in Kendal, Cumbria. His friend, the distinguished poet Kathleen Raine, who had lived part of her life in the northern counties, opened the exhibition.[6]

Whenever possible, Hubert attended the summer concerts at Sermoneta and at the Cistercian abbey of Fossanova, where St Thomas Aquinas died in 1274. Such was Hubert's love of music and admiration for his father-in-law's composition that he did all he could to promote Roffredo's music. Having secured from Schott's in Mainz the release of the copyright, he invited his niece Diane Howard to spend time with him at Ninfa sorting and cataloguing it; she then organised reprints of the main chamber works in London for distribution to conservatoires as well as to individual musicians. In 1978, Hubert invited the Gabrieli String Quartet, whom Diane managed in London, to perform two concerts at the Pontine Music Festival. As a preamble to their performance at the Caetani Castle up at Sermoneta, the members of this distinguished ensemble, at Hubert's request, played Roffredo's Second String Quartet privately in the *salone* of the villa. Hubert was moved to tears, saying that it was as if Roffredo were present in the room.

Hubert also found time to keep close to the wider Howard family. One recalls his pleasure at having been invited, not long after Lelia's death, to celebrate the memory of Henry Howard, 'Poet Earl' of Surrey. It was an occasion devised by Miles Fitzalan-Howard, 17th Duke of Norfolk, and it took place at Framlingham Castle, a seat of the Howards during the fifteenth and sixteenth centuries; it had belonged at one time to the unfortunate earl, and he is buried there.[7]

HUBERT LOVED animals and had a special empathy with the Ninfa dogs: the good-natured Orsetta, who was laid to rest in the flower border just the other side of the garden's green entrance gate; and Blackie, who used to howl at night and was both affectionate and excitable. In their time, each would follow him around the garden and into the surrounding countryside. Even as he aged, Hubert continued his practice of walking and climbing, often in the company of friends. The camaraderie and shared humour of the party members were reminiscent for Hubert of the many walks he had made with his brothers in Italy, including a trek from Rome to the Adriatic Sea.

Among the new group of fellow walkers were Cesare Tumedei, a distinguished lawyer and parliamentary deputy, and Johannes Schwarzenberg, the Austrian Ambassador to the Holy See, who, with his wife Kathleen, occupied the second-floor apartment of Palazzo Caetani; they were frequent guests at Ninfa. Tumedei often acted as nominal leader of these walking expeditions, once taking the party as far north as the Marche, close to where he was born. One can imagine them in the grandiose setting of the Sibillini Mountains, where once Tumedei led them up through the forests along the River Tenna, urging the party on with the prospect of a beer and a plate of pasta.

The walking companions were sometimes joined by Count Novello Cavazza, the architect and monument restorer, who oversaw works at the Palazzo Caetani and the restoration, after the deaths of Roffredo and Marguerite Caetani, of the villa at Ninfa. It was here, in a cupboard, that Hubert accumulated dozens of maps made by the Istituto Geografico Militare, covering all the Lazian hills and parts of the Abruzzo mountains. (A similar collection exists to this day in a drawer in his old bedroom at Lyulph's Tower, for his many hiking expeditions up into Cumbria's Northern Fells.) He would study such maps in detail, working out distance and elevation, and calculating, with unfailing accuracy, how long each walk would take. Known for his punctuality, he never allowed himself, or his party, to be late for a lunch.

Those who accompanied Hubert on his walks, even into his seventies, remembered how he would observe nature and how, at his measured pace, he seldom flagged. In her time, Lelia had looked askance at such endeavours, particularly if they involved his spending a night or two away. Lauro Marchetti recalls how Hubert set off with him early one morning on a bright June day. After a sandwich and a moment's rest on the summit of Monte Lupone, they continued to Segni, still moving north and away from Ninfa. There they rested in a chapel, before climbing up into the beech forests above the small town of Montelanico. They pitched a tent next to a watering hole but woke up the next morning to find themselves encircled by a herd of cows – more than Hubert had acquired for his dairy venture at Lyulph's Tower in the 1940s. With them, predictably, was a bull. For half an hour they were denied the call of nature, but made it back to Ninfa in perfect time for lunch. Even so, Lelia greeted them with the words, 'Siete pazzi!' ('You are out of your minds!').

As his appetite for long walks and his writings so often reveal, Hubert was profoundly moved by nature and the countryside. Besides plants, of which he developed a considerable knowledge, he loved birds. Fulco Pratesi recalls one of those ornithological high points on a climb with Hubert and Lauro, again to the summit of Monte Lupone. In his words:

It was a bright and beautiful day, and our aim was to see what we could of the fauna in this area. Among the species that interested us were two large birds of prey, in danger of extinction. The first was the golden eagle, whose nest on Mount Gemma had been looted by vandals who had left a hammer and sickle graffito on the site. The second was the very rare Egyptian Vulture, one of which was nesting on a rocky cliff just below the village of Norma. As we approached the summit, a magnificent specimen of the Vulture, black and white and with its distinctive yellow beak, a bird revered by the ancient Egyptians and found so often in their hieroglyphs, appeared in the sky. To the three of us, this seemed like an auspicious prophecy for the possible return of this species, now extinct throughout Italy, except for Sicily. This and other birdwatching expeditions with Hubert, including visits to WWF centres and habitats in the Tuscan Maremma, are tied to my memories of Hubert, who was one of the most important figures in the recent history of the Caetani and of Italian environmentalism.[8]

On 3 May 1981, during Ninfa's first major weekend opening of the year, Hubert penned a letter to his elder brother Francis, once more reflecting on the worries and joys arising from his work:

> The gardens here are in great beauty now, but yesterday, today and tomorrow they are open to the public, and this morning we had over 1,000 visitors, and there may be even more this afternoon. The pressures are terrifying – yet so many people longing to see something beautiful in a world always more arid, always more sterile. All the threats of taking away the waters of Ninfa and passing them over to industry are here again as the Cassa per il Mezzogiorno goes about draining the waters from above the lake … We had last weekend the assembly of the Italian Society for the Protection of Birds, of which I am honorary President, held at Latina and Sermoneta with a visit to Ninfa. A most rewarding occasion, with delegations from Turin to Palermo and fascinating conversations and discussions at a very high level, ending with the release of buzzards, falcons, owls and even a heron, all of which had been wounded by the satanic *cacciatori* [shooting parties] and brought back to health at the Society's hospital for birds at Parma. Some were released near the sea, at the lake of Fogliano, others in the woods of the National Park of the Circeo before an immense and fascinated audience of enthusiasts.[9]

As HE AGED, and perhaps because he was perceived to have almost the same status as the Caetani in his management of their patrimony,

Hubert became aware of a rather sycophantic tendency, on the part of lazy or fanciful travel writers, or those seeking favours, to exaggerate or to make wild assumptions about his status and title. Although in the line of the Dukes of Norfolk, who were historically close and, indeed, related to the English monarchy, Hubert's simple title of 'Honourable' was due to the fact that he was the son of a baron. In an Italian press article, Hubert was once described as the Duke of Norfolk; in another as a scion of Castle Howard in Yorkshire, a sumptuous estate that belongs to another branch of the Howard family. In his daily life, Hubert was often addressed as '*Eccellenza*' as well as '*Principe*' and other extravagant honorifics which he tolerated as a matter of courtesy. 'I really don't mind what they call me,' he once observed with resigned humour, 'although I draw the line at *Sua Santità*.'

In spite of the hard work, Hubert's life at Ninfa gave him many pleasures and benefits. He never disguised, for example, his delight at being able to eat the produce of the garden and of the farms: the honey; the avocado pears hanging abundantly in the walled garden from two lofty trees (planted after the war by his American mother-in-law); the luscious pomegranates; the kumquats and multiple varieties of citrus fruits adorning the walled garden. Having first tasted the nutritious kiwi fruit in a salad in London in the late 1970s, he later introduced them to Ninfa as a commercial crop, and felt able to declare in autumn 1986 that they had been adjudged 'among the best'. Perhaps his greatest comestible pleasure were the succulent Californian peaches, grown on the farm. One French guest at a Ninfa lunch party hosted by Hubert used to recall, with some bemusement, how Hubert had arranged to have brought into the dining room a lavish presentation of freshly picked peaches. While the guests watched in anticipation, Hubert proceeded to sample a small selection. They seemed ripe and juicy. But then, to the guests' dismay, Hubert declared them 'not quite ready' and the peaches were removed.

Although orderly and fastidious in his idiosyncratic way, Hubert loved the commotion of visiting nephews and nieces, taking them for walks up Monte Semprevisa or playing hide-and-seek with them in the garden.

One story that typifies his care and affection for them was his offer to take a ten-year-old great-nephew to a funfair in Rome. When they arrived, somewhere in the outskirts of the city, they found it closed. Hubert asked the little boy if there was anything else that might meet his heart's desire, to which the apparently simple answer was a banana. On that day, as Hubert used to delight in telling, there appeared to be not a single banana anywhere in Rome. The search, which lasted several hours, had to be abandoned. Hubert also used to tell the story of how he was doing the rounds of the garden and came across a tourist couple whose little boy, in a pushchair, was armed with a plastic pistol which he pointed at any bird he could see, shouting, 'Bam, bam!' Hubert approached the child and gently explained that Ninfa was a beautiful home to the birds and that no one should ever think of harming them. To the parents' chagrin, the child flung his harmless weapon into the river.

In early January 1983, Hubert treated a number of his nephews and their cousins to a memorable skiing holiday at the Château de Rougement in Gstaad, which had been booked by American friends. He described the party as 'Americanised Europeans and Europeanised Americans'. He felt he could no longer manage downhill skiing, so those who ventured up the mountain by funicular each day could look down on Hubert from a great height as he set off on his Norwegian skis, just as he had in wartime Finland. From Rougemont, on 8 January, he posted a letter to his brother Francis in which he speculated, with a touch of Catholic irony, that the Priory of Rougemont had been 'probably suppressed' and become, 'like the English monasteries, the property of some noble thief'. In his letter, he included a description of the socialist President Alessandro Pertini's visit to Ninfa on 18 December 1982:

I broke the ice when he arrived at Ninfa (in a suite of about fifteen cars and in terrible weather conditions) by expressing the hope that he would not get his feet wet. He spoke about everything, how the senators and deputies used to come into his park to shoot and how he had driven them all out telling them to shoot each other. He was most amusing and I think a terror to his escort.[10]

Hubert relaxing at the Château de Rougement, Gstaad, while
on a 1983 skiing holiday with family and friends

Another charming story accompanies Pertini's visit that day. Gabriella
Luchetti, one of the first councillors to serve the Roffredo Caetani
Foundation, had a special affection for Hubert, and he found her a source
of consolation after Lelia's death – indeed someone who mirrored Lelia's
gentleness and good taste. He trusted her, for example, to help him choose
replacement carpets for the castle, and she used to bring him little cakes
and keep him company. A day or two before Pertini's visit, Hubert asked
if she could help welcome him and provide a 'feminine touch', particularly
for the 'tea ritual'. Pertini mistook her for Hubert's wife and, as he was
leaving, asked whether, on his next visit, she might prepare him a plate
of fettuccine.[11]

One Sunday in June 1983, Hubert walked alone to the top of Monte
Semprevisa, bringing back with him some violet gentians, which, in his
humorous way, he named *Gentiani Semprevisa Howardii, ultra purpurea*.
He planted these in the rock garden at Ninfa, along with some 'yellow

viola, some Alyssum that seems gold and red, and other unusual precious little things'. Hubert had always derived pleasure from wild plants, but it was Lelia who taught him about gardening.[12]

In the following year, 1984, when Hubert was seventy-six, one began to sense that the pace of his life was beginning to tire him. He travelled to Lyulph's Tower for his summer holiday and, in a letter to Mondi dated 14 August, wrote of how badly he needed to rest after having entertained a large party of nephews and nieces, and revealing how much work was needed to keep Ninfa supplied with plants:

I went on resting and resting. There is always house administration, about which you know something. The poor old Tower has at last a new roof on it, with felting underneath, and all rotten timbers pulled out and substituted. A great and expensive work, but I am so pleased it is done. An even greater occupation has been my making up of lists of plants for the garden at Ninfa – a very precise and time-consuming and delicate pastime – with correspondence to nurseries, visits to gardens, consultations with experienced dendrologists and careful assessment of costs and transport facilities. I am going to be 77 so perhaps this will be the last great order for Ninfa, taking in consideration perhaps as many as 200 or more plants and finding out if and where they are available, and whether the Fireblight restrictions are likely to block any consignments sent from England through France to Italy.[13]

In spring 1985, from Ninfa, he wrote to Francis with further insights into the pace of his life:

I have had to prepare for the visit and lunch of about 20 people for Prince Charles and the Princess of Wales [the prince would later comment that Ninfa was the most beautiful thing he had experienced on his entire trip] and I am quite overwhelmed by the usual and many administrative problems ... I have planted all but about 300 of the plants that arrived safely from England, most of them in excellent condition and settling happily in their new environment.[14]

Although constantly worried that he might not be able to keep up the standards of the garden as Lelia would have wished, the work there, to judge by so many affirming letters and reports, was moving forward with promise. In the early 1980s, almost everything in the garden – particularly the watering – still had to be done by hand. Hand-pushed mowers and sickles were still the norm, and it was hard to keep up. Difficult decisions had to be made. At about this time, Hubert decided to create a small nursery garden to grow and nurture new species of plants to add to or replace Ninfa's already impressive stock. The call on manpower increased all the while and even Hubert used to say that he was getting 'very old', although the extraordinary amount he managed to accomplish belied that impression.

As public visits to Ninfa gathered momentum, Hubert commissioned one of his nephews to make what was probably the first ever film documentary on Ninfa. Mondi Howard wrote the commentary, except for the concluding passages. These were put into words by Hubert, who expressed once more his heartfelt concern about what 'the press of tourism' might one day do to Ninfa. The film was a long time in the making, but he saw it in the summer of 1986. The screening took place in the company of a small group of relatives gathered at a London film studio. Also present were his friends the poet Kathleen Raine and the artist Thetis Blacker. Hubert said that the film moved him very much.

When, two months later, Hubert was diagnosed with a terminal blood cancer, he took the news with resignation. He flew once more to England, staying with relatives in London and then moving north to wind down his affairs at the Tower. He broke the news to the author on the eve of his return to Italy. He was calm, measured and resigned. In Rome, the treatments began almost immediately. On 15 October, he wrote calmly to Francis about his situation:

I am not unduly worried by what has been told me. Indeed, in one sense, it is rather a privilege to know. Newman said growth is the only evidence of life. This is true both in a spiritual and in a physical sense ... I must say the world is the most beautiful place. Ninfa is more beautiful than ever, and full of butterflies that I have never seen before. We have been having lovely weather. Then I see all my friends here, and the people I work with, and humanity itself is of a divine quality. One must praise God for his creation, and His constant interest in us, and for the possibilities of rebirth and redemption.[15]

As news of his illness became more widely known, Hubert began to receive a flood of letters. They came from friends and every generation of his family – an enchanting testament to how much he was loved. On 12 December, a Friday, Mondi went out to Rome to be with Hubert, staying in the little guest apartment just above Palazzo Caetani's *piano nobile*. On the evening of his arrival, Mondi read to Hubert from the Psalms and from Fr John Dalrymple's book *Letting Go in Love: Reflections on Spiritual Formation*,[16] which did much to cheer him. The next morning Hubert's two doctors, Tafuri and Luciano, called in to report on the latest blood test and to prescribe new medicines. The side effect of one of these

Mondi and Francis together at Dean Farm for Francis' 80th birthday, 1985

was that Hubert found it hard to get any rest at night. He was, however, still able to dress and get up for lunch, to write letters and attend to business matters. Mondi wrote a diary of his stay in which he wondered, as many others were wondering, how Lelia's foundations could carry on as before without his brother's guiding hand, 'so prudent and sensitive,' and without his formidable knowledge of the family's history and patrimony.

After Sunday Mass at the nearby Church of the Gesù, Mondi accompanied the scholarly Padre GianPaolo Salvini, then editor of the old-established Jesuit *Civiltà Cattolica*, to Hubert's apartment so that he could administer the last rites. It was a short but intensely moving ceremony, with Hubert dressed and kneeling in the sitting room. Afterwards, Hubert gave Salvini a copy of the sermon that his Jesuit confrère, Fr Ronald Knox, had given on the occasion of his marriage to Lelia thirty-five years earlier. In the course of the next few days, as concern for Hubert mounted within the community of his Roman friends, Lauro Marchetti called in several times, as did Giacomo Antonelli and friends from Latina, who came with gifts for him. Hubert tired easily but was boosted at intervals by blood transfusions designed to recalibrate his blood count. Sadly, the cancer treatments did little to arrest the illness. It was a matter of living for the moment. He was cared for devotedly by his cook Gavina Casula, and her niece Jenny Malezyty. Mondi, before leaving Hubert on the morning of 18 December, thanked his dying brother for his fraternal love and care, and reassured him that his work for Lelia and the Caetani would have lasting impact. Hubert described his years with Lelia as the happiest of his life.[17]

On 23 December, his birthday, Hubert tendered his resignation from the Roffredo Caetani Foundation to take effect on 1 January 1987. He wished the councillors and employees a happy Christmas and prosperous New Year, explaining that after nine years at the helm a change was needed, although he mentioned that his decision was also for health reasons. He expressed confidence in the future of the foundation and heartfelt thanks to those who, with such dedication, had shared with him its great and important work.

During January 1987, as the illness worsened, Hubert was tenderly consoled at his apartment by sisters of the Spiritual Family 'The Work'.

This community of priests and sisters, whose main house is in Austria and whose official seat is in Rome, was founded by Mother Julia Verhaeghe (1910–97) and is based on the spirituality of St Paul. The foundress also considered the English Cardinal John Henry Newman to be a 'brother in spirit'. In 1975, Maria Katharina Strolz, then international superior of the sisters' community, found herself on a Rome-bound flight sitting next to the Vatican's papal nuncio to Belgium, Archbishop Igino Cardinale. She asked the archbishop if he knew of anyone in Rome who might be able to support the forthcoming Newman symposium there – the first of its kind. He responded by giving her Hubert's name. Hubert and Lelia duly helped sponsor the event, and so began a friendship. Newman had long been admired by Hubert, and was both a contemporary of Cardinal Edward Howard and a personal friend of Henry Fitzalan-Howard (1815–60), 14th Duke of Norfolk.[18]

Lelia and Hubert (front left) at the first Newman Conference, Rome, 1975

AT ABOUT this time, Hubert received a letter from Thetis Blacker.[19] She had come to know Hubert in the last years of his life, and had made several visits to Ninfa with Kathleen Raine. She wrote, in the full knowledge of his illness, of how Hubert had 'given and given during his wonderful life' and how it was largely through him and through his inspiration that Raine had been able to give the Temenos Academy to the world. Indeed, it was Blacker who wrote the words quoted on the frontispiece of this biography, from a subsequent letter of condolence to Mondi Howard: 'His greatness of spirit, his true nobility, his immense generosity, his courage and his strength and his gentleness all combined to make him one of the very greatest of men.'

Alessandro Onorati, lawyer, fine art expert and an original member of the council of the Camillo Caetani Foundation, was among friends and colleagues who called on Hubert in early January 1987. Hubert admitted to him in confidence that his pain had become severe. Knowing how pure and complete Hubert's faith was, Onorati gave him a little book by Blaise Pascal, entitled *Prayer to Ask of God the Proper Use of Sickness*, thinking it might be of some help. Hubert read it and thanked him.[20] Mondi, accompanied by Francis and the author, visited Hubert once more, and stayed several days, although by now it was just a question of time.

Malcolm Munthe, a friend from childhood, wrote these affectionate words in a letter that reached Hubert just a few days before he died:

> Hubert dear, your news makes me so sad. I think of our playing together with your brothers in Stockholm, as little children, when your father was in charge of the legation. I think of Palazzo Caetani and fairy-tale Ninfa and your beautiful Lelia, and I cannot believe I may not see you any more in this dear old world. I get happiness, at least, from the knowledge that your highly developed spirit has prepared you perfectly for this next great step of your life … I shall be thinking of you and praying for you as best I can.[21]

Friends in Rome, including the British Ambassador and his wife, Lord and Lady Bridges, rallied round. Hubert's condition worsened and on

14 February he was transferred to the Villa Flaminia Clinic. Early on
16 February the author, having received news of the worsening situation,
flew to Rome, arriving at the clinic that evening. Hubert, who had already
requested and been given Holy Communion, was being comforted by
Lauro Marchetti and several nurses. Giacomo Antonelli was also present.
On greeting him, Hubert opened his eyes and muttered with his unfailing
politeness, 'Esme, how good of you to come.' On his wall, he had asked
for a photograph of Lelia to be hung where he could see it. Lauro, who
in previous weeks had spent many hours at Hubert's side, devotedly kept
him company through the night and made a moving record of what took
place. Hubert died at dawn on the morning of 17 February.

HUBERT'S BROTHERS and close family flew out from England to be
present at a Mass celebrated for him the following day in a packed Santa
Maria in Campitelli. Many friends and representatives of the Pontine
communities attended. The author made a short tribute. Dame Iris Origo,
one of Hubert's oldest friends (whose great qualities as a writer had drawn
her close to the Caetani post-war literary milieu), added these words to
the many written tributes:

> Everyone who was present at the funeral service for Hubert Howard
> on 18 February in Santa Maria in Campitelli could not fail to be moved
> by the number of people attending it. Not only members of his own
> family and of the Roman aristocracy, but many country people from
> Ninfa and Sermoneta and others of the Roman *popolino*, a sign of the
> love which was felt for him by people of every age and class … I shall
> always remember his kindness and patience in Marguerite's last months
> when her mind began to fail and she could not bear to let Lelia out of
> her sight. After Marguerite's death he and Lelia continued her work
> together with equal enthusiasm and skill, and when Lelia too died
> prematurely Hubert continued it. On the last day on which I saw him,
> just before Christmas, he brought me a bunch of flowers from Ninfa

and described to me … the trees and climbing plants which Marguerite had planted [and which] had now grown into their full beauty … the concerts and seminars he was planning for Sermoneta in the summer, and [how Ninfa had become] a sanctuary for birds and other forms of wildlife … All this, however, only describes Hubert's works but does not do justice to the sweetness and generosity of his nature. His last weeks when he was often in great pain were spent in trying to ensure the future of Ninfa and that of his numerous dependants. Fully aware that there was no hope of recovery, he accepted his suffering with a truly Christian courage and fortitude, only asking his friends to pray for him. We are all impoverished by his loss but enriched by having had such a friend.[22]

Around a month later, on 25 March, in the capacious nave of Westminster Cathedral in London, another large crowd gathered for Hubert's memorial Mass. It was celebrated by Hubert's young friend, Fr Jock Dalrymple,[23] who had known him from his seminarian days in Rome in the mid-1980s. In addition to so many family members, friends and diplomats, representatives of the Prince and Princess of Wales, of the Italian Ambassador to London and of Europa Nostra, were present. Antonelli flew over from Rome to represent the two Caetani foundations.

Philip Howard, a nephew, read from Psalm 102. The gospel reading, so apt and comforting, was John 14:1–7, including this line: 'And if I go and prepare a place for you, I will come back and take you to be with me that you also may be where I am.' Another nephew, Anthony Howard, played the magnificent cathedral organ, and a great-nephew, Dominic Howard, read the bidding prayers.

In his address, Fr Dalrymple spoke of 'fidelity and simplicity' as being the hallmarks of Hubert's life and quoted from Hubert's valedictory letter to him, of September 1986:

Next year I shall be eighty and perhaps it is a useful reminder that I can no longer realise my own wishes and must submit, whether I like it or not, to an exterior destiny. When one is old, one moves slowly towards one's end, which gives one more time to think and pray.

The author gave the tribute, recalling Hubert's witness to the higher things in life: love and care for the poor, justice, peace, and civilisation itself. He recalled, too, Hubert's prodigious memory and curiosity, and how with his administrative orderliness he kept copious notes about the progress of his own illness.

In the days following Hubert's death the letters and tributes poured in. Tessa Bennett, a niece by marriage, wrote to Mondi as soon as she heard the news:

> I thought of Hubert's long and wonderfully full life and how much loved he has been and how much pleasure he has given by his company, which was so charming, and the steadiness his kind wisdom has brought and the beauty his care and attention has bestowed on places he loved, and I thought that one can't really be sad. There was no waste here, and he will be much missed because he was much loved, and real sadness lies in a life either cut off or wasted with no one to care. And Hubert was a good pilgrim and I am sure that all the trumpets sounded for him this morning.[24]

Kathleen Raine, in her letter of condolence to Mondi, wrote:

> I think of Hubert very often with sorrow, not for him for he is now with those he loved in the light of the divine presence … I remember we all read Dante together in Rome and Ninfa on one visit and Hubert quoted passages from the poet he understood so well. But Rome – Italy – for me is Hubert and Lelia … He was the most true, just, wise friend I ever had, but what has been surely is for ever.[25]

Sir Paul Wright, a distinguished former ambassador and great friend of the Howards, wrote to his godfather Mondi:

> I loved him, as I have loved all your family, for most of my life; and shall miss him for all his wonderful qualities: gentleness, honesty, sense of fun and of beauty … a great gentleman, a rare breed now, I fear, becoming endangered if not nearly extinct.[26]

Another letter came from Mondi's old Oxford University friend, 'Freddie' (by then Abbot Aelred) Sillem, of Quarr Abbey on the Isle of Wight. He wrote, 'I have always felt that Hubert was a kind of saint – and that isn't something I would say lightly of anyone.'[27] Echoing that sentiment, Malcolm Munthe's son Adam, one of Hubert's many godsons, wrote of Hubert that he was 'perhaps slightly misplaced from his proper position as one of those saints on the front of Notre Dame – wise, good and a little impatient'.[28]

James Lees-Milne, the diarist who had once depicted Hubert as a sort of entrenched old-world Catholic, resurfaced in a touching letter to Mondi, referring to Hubert thus:

A congenial friend, someone outstanding and sympathetic … reserved, though he had a delicious sense of humour and was so deeply serious underneath … a deeply pious man … He was unique. This is said of many but of him it is true.[29]

A distant cousin of Lelia, Oliver Impy, wrote to Mondi from Oxford:

Hubert was one of the most charming and kindly men one could ever meet … We had a wonderful day with him not so very long ago, looking for a Neolithic axe factory. It was pouring with rain, and Hubert had carried my very small daughter down a mountainside and was soaked. In the car we had all our bathing towels and we totally undressed Hubert and he sat in the car, steaming, wrapped up in multi-coloured towels, giggling happily.[30]

And from George Marylski, who hardly knew Hubert, came a memory which he shared with Mondi:

I am deeply stricken by the demise of Mr Howard, a wonderful person, so refined, cultured, so very kind, so delicate of feeling … one could not help but love him sincerely, just for that fascinating and so exceptional personality of his.[31]

Among many obituaries that followed Hubert's death was one written by Ivor Bulmer-Thomas for *Transactions*, a publication of the old-established Ancient Monuments Society in London, of which Hubert had been an Honorary Life Fellow. Bulmer-Thomas recalled how, on Hubert's prompting, the society had taken up several cases of conservation in Cumbria. Coincidentally, two letters, with a pertinent connection to monuments, arrived at Palazzo Caetani too late for Hubert to read them, and were rediscovered only recently. They were from the wife and daughter of Mason Hammond, the distinguished American classicist who became a friend of Marguerite Caetani and who had taught at the American Academy in Rome before the outbreak of World War II, and again throughout 1951. During the war, Hammond moved with the Allies from North America to Italy, where he was the first so-called 'Monuments Man', tasked with finding and salvaging important works of art that had been looted by the Germans. He and his family became regular visitors to Ninfa during his second assignment to the Academy. In 1959, Marguerite invited his daughter, Florence or 'Flossie', to fly over from America to help her with *Botteghe Oscure*. She lodged for a while with the American Ambassador James Dunn[32] and his family at Palazzo Caetani.

In her valedictory letter, Florence wrote:

Jack [her husband] and I were only just told by my parents how very ill you are and want to send this note of sympathy and great love … We do think of you often, always speak of you and Lelia when we walk near Francis and Katherine's house here [the Biddles were Katherine, Lelia's aunt, and her husband Francis], and we love knowing you are in that beautiful apartment in the palazzo, and I always love imagining you at Ninfa … I think back so often to that miraculous year (1959–60) when I lived with [Lexie, daughter of the Dunns] at the Dunns' apartment and helped Marguerite with her review. It was certainly one of the times in my life that remains like a shining jewel … totally clear and beautiful in my heart. Especially the days with you and Lelia and Marguerite, and Signor Bracco [Federico Bracco, the then administrator of Palazzo Caetani] racing down from Rome with some crisis or other for you to attend to. And are there still calla lilies in the river? And how I loved playing the pianos – in the palazzo and at Ninfa.[33]

The British-Italian Society in London also published a tribute in which John Vernon, Hubert's old friend from D Section in wartime Italy, wrote:

Hubert Howard will have a secure place in Roman annals because of what he did for one of the most famous and illustrious Roman families: to transmit to posterity virtually intact the centuries-old legacy of the Caetani. It was a remarkable economic, social and artistic feat. *Labor omnia vincit.*[34]

On 12 March, at St Andrew's Church in Greystoke, Cumbria, a second Requiem Mass was said for Hubert to allow the local community of his Cumbrian family and friends to remember him. It was celebrated by Fr Francis Hughes, a member of one of the Ullswater mountain rescue teams, whose Chapel of St Philip Howard in the lakeside village of Glenridding Hubert had helped to build. Francis and Mondi were present and were considerably to outlive Hubert, Francis dying in 1995 and Mondi in 2005. Henry, the youngest of the three brothers, had died of cancer in 1977, the same year in which Lelia died.

Hubert was buried in the sprawling Verano Monumental Cemetery in Rome, with family and friends in attendance. His place of rest, inside the imposing Caetani mausoleum, is next to Lelia and her family. On her tomb is engraved, 'Lelia Caetani, Gardener and Painter'. Hubert's bears no epitaph, though a suitable one might have been 'A Man for all Seasons'.

CHAPTER TEN

Labor Omnia Vincit

I T is said that one should measure a man less by what he achieves
than by who he is. In looking back on Hubert's life, one cannot help
but be struck by his personal courage. This is evident in the way he
embraced and dealt with periods of disillusionment and introspection as
a younger man, and beyond these the 'grand' causes in which he believed
(played out in wartime Finland and Italy, and by his unfaltering commitment to conserving the Caetani patrimony). As we have seen, Hubert was
guided from an early age by an uncompromising sense of right and wrong.
In this, one might say that he was a worthy bearer of the Howard family
motto 'Sola Virtus Invicta' ('Virtue Alone is Unconquered'). It was virtue,
surely, that defined him and led to his early, idealistic view of the world,
and to those periods of existential melancholy, although these ceased as
soon as he found happiness and fulfilment with Lelia.

All such defining personal qualities were, however, the basis of a work
ethic that never faltered. In this he exemplified the motto that gives title
to this chapter and which was quoted by Hubert's friend, John Vernon,
in tribute to him. Hubert's world may for a while after Lelia's death have
seemed bleak and lonely, but he found a way of resuming his work with
renewed vigour and hope.

While Hubert was the first to say that most of his life's accomplishment
was owing to his good fortune in having married Lelia, his efforts, as
the last 'family' chairman of the two major Caetani foundations, bore

fruit beyond his imaginings. During Hubert and Lelia's lifetime both had grown and been transformed. Since Hubert's death, the work of the Camillo Caetani Foundation has matured and expanded still more, the family archives being now a hub of scholarly activity carried out with imagination and to the highest standards. In the country, the Roffredo Caetani Foundation's work of culture and conservation, centred on the garden of Ninfa and the Caetani Castle at Sermoneta, would have pleased Hubert and Lelia no less.

The fabled garden, once as it were wrapped for its own protection in a veil of mystery, enjoys high international visibility these days. In February 2000, it gained the status of a 'Natural Monument' by decree of the governing body of the Lazio region. Being at once an important form of regional protection and a further validation of Ninfa's true importance as a model of good conservational practice, this designation is deeply significant today. In recent years, too, the garden has won several prestigious international awards, and its appeal has grown stronger each year, both in Italy and abroad. As in the past, however, this pearl of the Caetani patrimony has found itself in the path of new challenges and threats. It is debatable, for example, how Hubert might have reacted to the

A meeting of the general council of the Roffredo Caetani Foundation, Ninfa, 2019

extraordinary millennial boom in demand for public visits to Ninfa, and to the fact that, in contrast to his own perhaps overly cautious projection that the garden could not sustain visitor numbers of above 45,000 annually, such numbers have long since been surpassed.

And yet his caution was well grounded, for two very specific reasons. The first of these was attributable to Lelia's testamentary desire that the garden continue to be conserved 'perfectly, according to the traditions of the past'. This does at the very least mandate caution, the more so when one considers that this unique place was conceived by its makers as a sanctuary, an oasis, to be nurtured by sensitive hands and with the utmost respect for its vulnerable ecosystem. Since its early twentieth-century incarnation as a garden, Ninfa has always prospered according to its own terms of reference, its beauty alone sufficient to spread the gospel that this is a wondrous and idyllic place to visit – as much a balm for the senses as a showcase for plants, vistas and monuments from a bygone age. It cries out to be left untouched by contemporary whims or fancies, never to be exploited, and never to be disassociated from those who conceived it, nurtured it and, above all, understood it. Even before the garden came into existence, the ruins of that once bustling medieval town – a haunting necropolis choked by weeds and ivy, and yet adorned with spontaneous flowering – were a magnet for scholarly explorers. They came in considerable numbers, among them the German historian Ferdinand Gregorovius, who famously described Ninfa as 'the Pompeii of the Middle Ages', and intrepid English writers and painters such as Edward Lear, Augustus Hare and Richard Bagot. As an appeal to the Romantic imagination, the Ninfa of 150 years ago would have been hard to surpass.

The second reason was more pragmatic. It is that only twelve of the garden's twenty acres are accessible to large numbers. To avoid damage to the lawns, members of the public are nowadays asked to stick to the footpaths, a combined surface area of less than one fifth of the accessible whole. The foundation has done well to accommodate higher levels of visitors without lasting ill effects. Such achievement also owes much to the modernisation, since Hubert's time, of managerial and communication techniques, and the use of digital systems for attracting, booking and handling large numbers – a far cry from Hubert's earliest days trying to manage the country estates without a computer or even a telephone. It is surely ironic that beautiful Ninfa, at times so threatened by the forces of 'progress and profit', is now worth its weight in gold within the Pontine economy, providing employment for many and filling local hotels and restaurants with visitors, particularly in the spring and summer seasons.

Such security, peace and quiet as Ninfa has been able to enjoy thanks to Hubert and Lelia's efforts in the 1960s and 1970s were, however, placed in jeopardy at the turn of the century by a hotly contested battle to have Rome's third airport sited along the Appian Way – just three miles from the garden. Seen from the perspective of Latina's business community, this might have been a prestigious coup linking Latina to London and other European capitals at a stroke, while at the same time enticing new waves of tourists to Latina's lidos and further south to sport themselves on the pristine dunes and beaches of Sabaudia and Monte Circeo. Seen, however, from the perspective of a conservationist and a lover of Ninfa, this was an unimaginable danger. One knew this from a single experimental take-off and landing of a Boeing 727 from the small military airbase (the proposed site), on a stretch of land that had once belonged to Gelasio Caetani. That thunderous sound, rebounding off the hill above Ninfa, came as a shock to those who were in the garden that day. It sounded like a death knell for Ninfa. Happily this soon fell silent, following a political decision to site the airport elsewhere.

However, as surely as Hubert and Lelia and the early councils of the country foundation could not have foreseen the phenomenal rise in public demand to visit the garden, still less could they have imagined the increasing impact upon it of global warming, or indeed the as yet unmeasurable but potentially adverse effects of a worldwide pandemic. In the thirty-four years since Hubert's death, the garden has never been more vulnerable to the random forces of nature. Such forces have included hill fires that have descended to within a few yards of the garden's eastern boundaries; a localised storm and landslide so severe that it eviscerated the river, spewing mud and sediment all over the garden and drowning sheep in a nearby field; and in 2017 a drought that lasted eight months – enough to spark a minor regional emergency. As any gardener knows, the loss of trees and plants to the elements is no less painful than their loss to old age and disease.

Just as water gave birth to Ninfa (so named after the water nymphs that were believed to inhabit its springs), so it remains its lifeline. It is therefore worrying that over the thirty years since the Roffredo Caetani Foundation began taking a more serious approach to the monitoring of local hydrological trends, and comparing its findings with those of the regional authorities, the Lepini water table, on which Ninfa depends, has been in decline. The drought of 2017 resulted in a drop of more than one metre in the level of Ninfa's historic man-made lake. The otherwise sparkling and lively river that flows from it and makes its way through the garden, and on whose banks generations of admirers have gathered over the years, became shallow and sluggish. The old stone water canals, stretching from the lake to the arboreta, dried up completely and Ninfa's automated irrigation system ceased to function. One can imagine Hubert's earnest rhetoric at some hypothetical conference or other, having perhaps to describe entering the garden, once so alive and refreshing – and seeing the lawns scorched, and no longer hearing the agreeable babble of Roffredo Caetani's little streams and waterfalls. This period was not only a worrying reminder of the garden's vulnerability, if such were needed, but also a call to more concerted action at a regional level.

In addition to the quality of today's stewardship of Ninfa and its recognition as one of the most important gardens in the world, Hubert and Lelia would have been delighted by the 200-acre park and wetland, adjacent to the garden, a project that germinated in 2002. The area, known as 'Pantanello', has a number of small lakes and ponds teeming with seasonal aquatic birds. Around it is extensive new woodland – a sought-after habitat for pheasant, foxes, badgers and wild boar. The inspiration behind Pantanello was the idea of recreating a small stretch of the original Pontine Marshes, devoid of the once infamous mosquito.

View across the Pantanello Park at Ninfa

The area is equipped with hides and walkways for the visiting public, and is also a centre for the study of biodiversity. The project, in its historical symbolism as well as in its innovative contribution towards the expansion of parkland in the region, would have delighted Hubert and Lelia, and they might even have deemed it an extension of their own imaginations – surely a posthumous gift to them both.

Another positive development, that would further have gladdened their hearts, has been the emergence of the foundation's local headquarters, in the hamlet of Tor Tre Ponti, as a unique and vibrant cultural centre within the Pontine area. In its eighteenth-century buildings are to be found a growing archive of historic documents, a permanent exhibition of Lelia's paintings, and facilities for research and conferences. Culture is at the heart of the Caetani legacy, and this carries on not only in the annual Pontine Music Festival, hosted and sponsored by the foundation, but in the many cultural events that it organises, and the books and publications with which it is associated. Since the enlightened and dynastic Caetani first came to prominence in the region in late medieval times, they have shaped and massively influenced the entire Pontine and Lepini tradition.

To this day they are the inexhaustible historic and cultural resource on which the Caetani foundations depend.

Hubert always had in mind the possibility of creating one day an international association of admirers and benefactors of Ninfa. Formed in England in 2005, from where it is administered, the International Friends of Ninfa shares the broad conservational goals of the Roffredo Caetani Foundation, which it supports in a number of ways that include financial grants, professional advice and co-sponsorship of publications. Such was the love and hospitality shown in their time by Hubert and Lelia to so many, and such has been the impact of Ninfa on the legion of visitors since their day, that hundreds flocked to become members, including some whose names stand tall in the firmament of contemporary gardening and conservation. A particular pleasure for them both would have been the presence of younger generations of their own families. Such connections are yet another part of their legacy, a bond of familial continuity.

The picture gallery at Tor Tre Ponti, with a permanent exhibition of Lelia's paintings

A group of the International Friends of Ninfa walking beside the river, spring 2009

A MILD-MANNERED opponent of the polluters and harbingers of ugliness, to some a seemingly old-fashioned gentleman and to others a man who embodied an unusual mixture of otherworldliness and dogged pragmatism, Hubert may at times have been derided for his vision, for his values and for his work. However, as Italian conservationists have roundly acknowledged, Hubert's judgement was sound, his actions transformative. Indeed, in the various tributes that appeared in Italian and English newspapers, Hubert was variously described as 'a grandee of the Agro Pontino', 'the Father of the Oasis of Ninfa' and even 'the man who saved the beauty of Italy'. History will no doubt bury such well-intentioned honorifics. For, besides Lelia's love and the love of his friends and family, which was never lacking, Hubert wanted nothing more than that his life's work in conservation be of some value.

The facts surely speak for themselves. Not only did Hubert oversee the vitally important transition of the Caetani patrimony from one kind of ownership to another, but he also prepared the ground for an unknowable future, and this as we have seen has already borne fruit beyond his imaginings. All this he accomplished with unswerving loyalty to Lelia and her family, and out of his love of Italy. Hubert can thus rest in the sure knowledge that his work has made a lasting difference.

Notes

ABBREVIATIONS FOR ALL THE NOTES

CCF Camillo Caetani Foundation
RCF Roffredo Caetani Foundation
HFA Howard Family Archives

CHAPTER ONE: THE TOWER BY THE LAKE

1 Esme Howard, 1st Baron Howard of Penrith (1863–1939). Served in diplomacy from 1885 to 1930, with some intermissions for travel and adventure. His postings were many and varied, including Washington (two tours), Hungary, Sweden and Switzerland. His career culminated with six years as British Ambassador to Washington, from 1924 to 1930. He was raised to the peerage on his retirement in 1930.

   The name Esme is uncommon in the masculine form. It derives from the French 'Aimée' (meaning loved or esteemed one) and was used by the French court panegyrists to describe Mary Stuart (1542–87), Queen of Scots, in childhood. Mary in turn gave this name in the masculine form to her godson Esme Stuart, 1st Duke of Lennox. The Howard family can, however, lay some direct claim to it by reason of the marriage, in 1625, of Lady Elizabeth Stuart (daughter of Esme Stuart, 3rd Duke of Lennox) to Henry Frederick Howard, 22nd Earl of Arundel, Surrey and Norfolk, and grandson of Saint Philip Howard. Of their twelve children, their youngest son, born in 1645, was the very first Esme Howard in history. Like his forebears, Hubert's father never used an acute accent on the final 'e' of 'Esme'.

2 Bonaldo Stringher (1907–99) was one of Italy's foremost conservationists. He was Hubert's exact contemporary, a founding member with him of Italia Nostra, and among the first councillors to be appointed to the RCF.

3 Hubert's brothers: Esme ('Esmetto') (1903–26), Francis (1905–99), Edmund ('Mondi') (1909–2005), and Henry (1913–77).

4 James ('George') Lees-Milne (1908–97) was an English writer and expert on country houses, who worked for the National Trust from 1936 to 1973. He was an architectural historian, novelist, diarist and biographer. His observations on Hubert are from *A Mingled Measure: Diaries 1953–1972* (John Murray, 1994), 231. (James Lees-Milne Papers. General Collection,

Beinecke Rare Book and Manuscript Library, Yale University.) Lees-Milne's wife, Alvilde, was a well-known garden writer, and admirer of the celebrated Caetani garden of Ninfa about which she wrote a piece in the spring 1988 edition of *Hortus*.

5 The *Apologia Pro Vita Sua* (1865) is St John Henry Newman's great spiritual defence of his life's work. It was written in response to provocation in Oxford academic circles at the time he converted to Roman Catholicism in 1845. He was one of the nineteenth century's greatest English theologians, thinkers and churchmen.

6 *Theatre of Life*, Lord Howard of Penrith's two-part autobiography (Hodder & Stoughton, 1935–6), ii, 625.

7 The Lake Poets were part of the English Romantic Movement. William Wordsworth (1770–1850), Samuel Taylor Coleridge (1772–1834) and Robert Southey (1774–1843) were among the leading members. At different times they all lived in the Lake District, but each had different notions as to what the Lakes represent.

8 Quotations regarding Charles Howard, 10th Duke of Norfolk, are from Chapter 11, 'The Greystoke Dukes', in John Martin Robinson's *The Dukes of Norfolk: A Quincentennial History* (Oxford University Press, 1982), 166–84.

9 Ibid.

10 From Wordsworth's *Guide to the Lakes* (5th edition, 1835), ed. Ernest de Sélincourt (Oxford University Press, 1906, repr. 1977), 108.

11 Coleridge's description of Lyulph's Tower is from his 1799 Notebook in *The Notebooks of Samuel Taylor Coleridge* (Princeton, 1957), i, edited by Kathleen Coburn.

12 On Hubert's death in 1987, Lyulph's Tower became the property of Philip, 3rd Baron Howard of Penrith (b. 1945). There, he has carried on with works of maintenance and restoration, and has created a remarkable garden in the Japanese style.

CHAPTER TWO: ESME AND ISABELLA

1 Esme Howard's family is related to the Carnarvons through the marriage of his aunt Henrietta Molyneux-Howard to Henry Herbert, 3rd Earl of Carnarvon, in 1830; and of his sister Elizabeth ('Elsie') who, in 1878, became the second wife of Henry, 4th Earl of Carnarvon. Elsie's son Aubrey, a brave and enterprising man whose exploits were beautifully chronicled in his granddaughter Margaret Fitzherbert's book *The Man who was Greenmantle* (Oxford University Press, 1985), was therefore a half-brother of George Herbert, 5th Earl of Carnarvon, world famous for having sponsored the expedition that discovered King Tutankhamen's tomb in 1922. Elsie's husband, Henry, inherited the magnificent Villa Alta Chiara, at Portofino, the name derived from one of the best-known Carnarvon properties in

England, Highclere Castle, in Hampshire. Henry died in 1890, she in 1929. It was at another Herbert property, Tetton House in Somerset, that Hubert and Lelia's wedding reception took place in 1951.

2 *Theatre of Life*, i, 209–10.

3 Prince Sigismondo Giustiniani Bandini (1818–1908) became Hubert's maternal grandfather.

4 Palazzo Bandini in Via del Sudario in Rome. The imposing building, first named after Bernardo Caffarelli who built it, was designed by a pupil of Raphael in the late sixteenth century. It passed to Cardinal Vidoni in 1816 and to the Bandini family in 1886. They held on to it for three decades. Before World War I, the palazzo became the German Embassy and was afterwards appropriated by the Italian fascists.

5 B. J. C. McKercher's *Esme Howard: A Diplomatic Biography* (Cambridge University Press, 1989), 32–3.

CHAPTER THREE: ANCESTRAL TRACES

1 Jessie Childs' biography of the 'Poet Earl', *Henry VIII's Last Victim: The Life and Times of Henry Howard, Earl of Surrey* (Jonathan Cape, 2006), is one of the best contemporary accounts of the earl's life, and includes a comprehensive evaluation of his work as a poet.

2 This quotation is from the epilogue of Neville Williams' biography *Thomas Howard: Fourth Duke of Norfolk* (Barrie and Rockliff, 1964), 257. Hubert read this book at Ninfa as soon as it came out, and made copious notes.

3 Vitale II Michiel (d. 1172), Doge of Venice, ruled during an important crisis in the Venetian Republic's relations with the Byzantine Empire. His assassination led to a significant revision of the Venetian constitution. He tried to maintain good relations with the Western emperor Frederick Barbarossa, who, in 1159, with the connivance of the Colonna family (old rivals of the Caetani), attempted to thwart the conclave that had elected Pope Alexander III (Rolando Bandinelli). The pope then fled to Ninfa (already a papal fiefdom and later to become part of the Caetani estates), where he was consecrated in its principal church of Santa Maria Maggiore.

4 The curious story of the marriage between the monk Nicolò Giustiniani and Anna, the doge's daughter, appears on several websites, e.g. 'How the family Giustinian was saved', 15 Dec 2010 post from *The Other Venice* blog: <https://the-other-venice.tumblr.com/post/2323514478>.

5 Cecilia Giustiniani (1796–1877) and Carlo Bandini (1779–1850) were Hubert's maternal great-grandparents.

6 Pius X's gentle admonishment of Maria Cristina Giustiniani Bandini was a reflection on the Catholic attitude to women in those days. Her personality must have been formidable for him to have changed his mind.

7 The term 'black nobility' is most often associated with the aristocratic Italian families that sided with Pius IX when, in 1870, the Papal States were seized by the royal army led by the Savoyards. In reality, it has existed for centuries, originating in the baronial class of Rome and in the powerful families who moved to the capital to benefit from their connection to the papacy. They supported the popes in the governance of the Papal States and in the administration of the Holy See. Among families that once belonged to the black nobility were the Caetani. During the Risorgimento, Michelangelo Caetani, 13th Duke of Sermoneta, supported the creation of a united Italy, and in consequence the family became 'white', or secular, nobility.

8 The Newburgh earldom, which may appear unusual since the title is Scottish, came into the family with Vincenzo Giustiniani, sixth earl, who died in 1826. It was first created, in the Scottish peerage, for James Livingston who became Viscount Newburgh in 1647 and Earl of Newburgh in 1660.

CHAPTER FOUR: BETWEEN THE WARS

1 See McKercher's *Esme Howard: A Diplomatic Biography*, 163.

2 Thomas à Kempis (1380–1471) concluded the four books of the *Imitation of Christ* in 1420, as a personal and private guide to the spiritual life. Kempis had written the original in Latin.

3 Account based on Chapter 19 of *Theatre of Life*, ii, 464–84.

4 The author and lifelong friend of Hubert, Dame Iris Origo (1902–88), wrote of this first encounter in her tribute to Hubert following his death in 1987 (see Chapter 9, 141–2). Origo was a distinguished writer who, with her husband Marchese Antonio Origo, turned their Tuscan estate, La Foce, into one of the finest gardens of Italy, now known also for its annual summer music festival Incontri in Terra di Siena.

5 Hubert's correspondence from Cambridge and the Salzburg diaries and letters/HFA.

6 Ibid.

7 The Catholic Worker Movement began as a lay Roman Catholic initiative in the USA and Canada. It espoused the principles of personal reform, care for the poor and absolute pacifism. For a while it attracted a significant number of young, thoughtful and idealistic Catholics, including not just Hubert but also his brother Mondi and many of their friends.

8 Franklin D. Roosevelt (1882–1945), thirty-second president of the USA, was known as FDR, and was a fifth cousin of Theodore Roosevelt, whom Esme Howard and his elder sons got to know during the former's first posting to Washington from 1907 to 1909.

9 The Chapins were a distinctive Non-Conformist English family when they settled in America in the mid-eighteenth century, subsequently making their

fortune in railways. Adèle Alsop was the daughter of Reese Denny Alsop of New York, a maritime lawyer, and his wife, Julia Chapin. Julia was the daughter of Robert Williams Chapin, the younger brother of Marguerite Chapin's father, Lindley Hoffman Chapin.

10 See McKercher's *Esme Howard: A Diplomatic Biography*, 1.

11 The encounter with Mussolini appears in *Theatre of Life*, ii, 605–7.

CHAPTER FIVE: OSASTO SISU AND THE FINNISH DEBACLE

1 Quotation from Hubert's Winter War diaries/HFA.

2 Extracts from newspaper cuttings among Hubert's Winter War papers/HFA.

3 Kermit Roosevelt (1889–1943), a son of US President Theodore Roosevelt, explored two continents with his father, was a Harvard University alumnus, and a soldier who served in two world wars with both the British and the American armies. He was also a businessman and a writer. He fought a lifelong battle with poor health, depression and alcoholism, and eventually took his own life.

4 From Hubert's Winter War diaries/HFA.

5 Ibid.

6 The 1918 to 1919 civil war in Finland pitted an alliance of 'Red' Finns and Bolshevik Russians against the 'White' forces, led by Mannerheim, of the legitimate government. The success of the White forces ensured the independence of Finland from Russian influence. Towards the end of his mandate in Sweden, Esme Howard encountered Mannerheim and his agents on a number of occasions, at which Britain's support for the Whites was sought and, with Esme Howard's advocacy, eventually given although conditional on Finnish neutrality, particularly in respect of Germany.

7 Colville ('Collie') Barclay (1913–84) was well known to the Howards. His father succeeded Esme Howard as Britain's envoy to Sweden in 1919 and 'Collie' was a pre-World War II contemporary of Hubert's at the Foreign Office. Date of letter unknown.

8 From Justin Brooke's *The Volunteers*, 101. Brooke, one of the original party members, contacted Hubert in 1984, seeking his help in order to write a book about the British Expeditionary Force. Hubert not only sent him valuable information but also read the manuscript and, in September 1984, met some of the aging volunteers in Salisbury. The book was published in 1990 under the title *The Volunteers: The Full Story of the British Volunteers in Finland, 1939–41*. In a letter to Brooke of 25 September 1985, Hubert congratulated the author and, harking back to that 'extraordinary episode', confessed that when Brooke first approached him about the book, he had wondered about the usefulness of rehearsing once again the frustration and bitterness of such a human and historic failure. He added: 'the memory of it remains like

an existentialist nightmare evoked by the brain fever of a Sartre'. Brooke's dedication of the book, appropriately, was: 'To the brave people of Finland, who, despite all their difficulties, endured us as well.'

9 From Hubert's draft notes/HFA.

10 As related by Hubert to Lauro Marchetti, who was employed by the Roffredo Caetani Foundation in 1972, and worked closely with Hubert and Lelia at Ninfa for many years.

11 Hubert's letter is dated 5 August 1940/HFA.

12 The widowed Anne Bazley (née Hotham) married Hubert's elder brother Francis, Lord Howard of Penrith, in 1947, after his return from Germany as a wounded prisoner of war. Hubert's letter is dated 10 May 1941/HFA.

13 Hubert's letter to Haskell is dated 21 October 1941/HFA.

14 For security reasons, perhaps, Hubert did not specify to which shipping company he was referring, but it was probably the Johnson Line, whose owner had become a great friend of Hubert's father and mother in Stockholm during World War I.

15 Vessey's poem is undated/HFA.

16 Malcolm Munthe (1910–95), who had been wounded during the Finnish War, went on to fight with the British military in the Italian campaign, and was again wounded, this time at Anzio. He received the Military Cross (MC) for bravery. He was a conservationist and lover of Italy, who lived for many months each year at his Castello di Lunghezza, outside Rome. When he retired, it was to look after his various homes in England, and his fine collection of paintings. He remained a lifelong friend of Hubert and his family.

17 Victor Mallet (1893–1969) saw military service in World War I and held a number of diplomatic postings between the two world wars, the last of which was as British envoy to Sweden (1940–45), where he met Hubert. From 1947 to 1953, Mallet served as British Ambassador to Rome, where he again met Hubert, and Mondi, who was serving by that time at the embassy.

CHAPTER SIX: BROTHERS AT WAR

1 Major Gustavus ('Gus') March-Phillipps (1902–42) appears in Francis Howard's handwritten summary of his experience on two commando raids, in HFA. Number 62 Commando was a secret unit set up to strike at the Germans. It was brought into being by Winston Churchill. Some have suggested that March-Phillipps may have been the inspiration for James Bond: 'Was the Gunner Buried on Omaha Beach the Original 007?', *The Observation Post*, 19 Jan 2015: <https://www.theobservationpost.com/blog/?p=1172>

2 Claude Auchinleck (1884–1981) gained some distinction in World War II as the commander responsible for halting the German offensive at El Alamein in the Western Desert.

3 Stuart Carter Dodd (1900–75) was an American sociologist and educator, who published research on the Middle East and on mathematical sociology, and who was a pioneer in scientific polling. He published his findings after the war in his 'Towards World Surveying' (1946) which appeared in *Public Opinion Quarterly*, 10(4), 470–83. He became famous for being the only pollster to predict that President Harry S. Truman would defeat Governor Thomas E. Dewey in the 1948 presidential elections. Dodds was even called to testify before Congress and explain how he had managed to be right.

4 General Harold Alexander (1891–1969) was one of the most successful British generals in World War II. In November 1944, he became Commander-in-Chief of all Allied forces in Italy.

5 Carlo Sforza (1872–1952) and Alberto Tarchiani (1865–1964) were to become key to Italy's post-war political identity as shaped in no small measure by the efforts of Allied intelligence. Sforza had been appointed Italian Ambassador to France in 1922, resigning only nine months later in protest at Mussolini's rise to power. His anti-fascist stance in the Italian Senate eventually forced him into exile, in 1926. Head of the many Italian political exiles at that time was Carlo Rosselli (1899–1937), leader of the Giustizia and Libertà movement, who was brutally assassinated in France in 1937. With Rosselli no more, Sforza became *de facto* head of the resistance in exile, moving from one country to another and writing critiques of fascist ideology and Italian appeasement. He was to become one of the architects of post-war Italian politics, serving in the cabinet of Alcide de Gasperi (1881–1954) from 1947 to 1951. His friend, Alberto Tarchiani, a founder of Giustizia and Libertà, had studied at Rome's La Sapienza University and taken to journalism in 1903, volunteering for military service with the Italian army in World War I. Following Hitler's invasion of France in 1940, he moved to New York and became secretary of the anti-fascist Mazzini Society. After the fall of Italian fascism, effectively with the signing of the September 1943 Armistice, he joined the government of Pietro Badoglio (1885–1964) as Minister of Public Works. When Rome fell in June 1944, Tarchiani moved seamlessly into the cabinet of Italy's new prime minister, the veteran politician Ivanoe Bonomi (1873–1951), as minister of National Reconstruction. From 1945 to 1955, he served as Italian Ambassador to Washington.

6 John Vernon was an early D Section friend of Hubert and Mondi, who kept up with them both after the war. He met his future wife Susanna in Rome before the war and married her on 21 May 1949. Her father was the distinguished General Bolesław Wieniawa-Długoszowski, appointed Polish

Ambassador to Rome in 1938. The Polish Embassy at that time was located in Palazzo Caetani (32, Via delle Botteghe Oscure) with the result that before the war, John and Susanna came to know Roffredo (whose maternal grandmother was Polish) and Marguerite Caetani, socialising with them in Rome and at Ninfa. The embassy closed on 13 June 1940, on news that Italy had sided with Germany. John and Susanna left Rome at the same time, but John returned to Italy and joined PWB's D Section in 1943. He often encountered the Howard brothers and kept up with them throughout his later life. John and Susanna's son, Dr Gervase Vernon, sheds further light on PWB activities through his writings and letter compilations (for example *Love Letters in a Time of War*, 2020) which traces the personal correspondence between his parents from 1940 to 1958.

7   Bernard Wall (1908–74), Catholic intellectual and writer, Italophile and friend of the Howards. He first gave his account of Via Po in October 1972 as part of a congress organised by Ian Greenlees under the auspices of the British Institute in Florence. His paper was entitled 'Via Po Days' and the subject of the congress was 'England and Italy in the 20th Century'.

8   Ian Greenlees (1913–88), a larger-than-life figure, had taken over the British Institute in Rome just before war broke out. A man of erudition and culture, and greatly knowledgeable about Italy, he became prominent in Allied intelligence with PWB during the war (see Note 7 above). In 1958, he was appointed director of the British Institute in Florence, where he remained until his retirement in 1980. Greenlees got to know Hubert well and was a founding member of the Italian League for Bird Protection (LIPU), equivalent to the Royal Society for the Protection of Birds (RSPB). It was formed in 1965.

9   Umberto Saba (1883–1957), Emilio Cecchi (1884–1966), Giuseppe Ungaretti (1888–1970), Mario Soldati (1906–99), Elsa Morante (1912–85), and Alberto Moravia (1907–90) were all distinguished Italian writers and academics bound together by their common anti-fascism. The power of their pens made them natural allies of PWB. (For Carlo Sforza see Note 5 above.)

10   Piero Calamandrei (1889–1956), author, soldier, Florence University professor and politician. Hubert's personal account of the liberation of Florence is also cited briefly in the English historian Christopher Hibbert's magnificent *Florence: The Biography of a City* (Viking, 1993), 302–3.

11   From Mondi Howard's war diary/HFA. Although Mondi kept up with Jane McLean after the war, and she once came over from America to visit him following his retirement in 1969, it has been impossible to find further information about her.

12   Henry Howard's movements in Italy appear in the author's autobiographical work *Virtues and Vanities* (MPG Books, 2012) and are derived from a

number of sources, including the memories of Henry's late wife Adèle and her family.

13 Hubert's movements in this period can be traced among other sources to letters in the HFA sent during his home leave (Christmas and New Year 1944–5) to Mondi, who was still active in Italy with D Section.

CHAPTER SEVEN: HUBERT AND LELIA

1 Edward, 1st Baron Skelmersdale (1771–1853); his granddaughter Ada Bootle-Wilbraham (1846–1934). The Bootle-Wilbraham family's baronetcy of Skelmersdale goes back to the late eighteenth century and was held, between 1880 and 1930, by the Earls of Lathom.

2 Onorato Caetani (1842–1917), 14th Duke of Sermoneta, inherited the family dukedom in 1883. He was a multilinguist and had an abiding interest in geography and music. He became a member of the Italian Parliament in 1870, before becoming mayor of Rome in 1890. Like his father, Michelangelo Caetani (1804–82), the polymath 13th Duke of Sermoneta, said to be the cleverest man in Italy, Onorato was an intellectual and artist. He inherited his father's anticlericalism, and distaste for the so-called 'black nobility' of which, ironically, Hubert's Bandini relatives had been a conspicuous part (see Chapter 3, Note 7).

3 Leone Caetani (1869–1935), Onorato and Ada's eldest son, succeeded his father as fifteenth duke. Like his forebear Onorato Caetani (1542–92), he married a member of the Colonna family, centuries-old rivals of the Caetani. Her name was Vittoria Colonna (1880–1954). The marriage took place in 1901, but his melancholy disposition was unsuited to her lively and gregarious personality and they soon separated. Leone, a deputy of the Italian Parliament from 1909 to 1913, is most remembered for his remarkable contribution to the study of Islam, and his decision to leave Italy with his mistress and daughter Sveva, and find a new life in Canada. Leone and Vittoria's only son, Onorato, succeeded to the dukedom in 1935 but died in 1946.

4 Roffredo Caetani (1871–1961) became 17th Duke of Sermoneta in 1946 on the death of his nephew Onorato. His work as a composer and performer was concentrated around a few years, reaching a peak in *c.* 1909. From 1887 to 1904 he had limited himself to instrumental music, composing not only twenty works for piano but also chamber and symphonic music. Then, between 1910 and 1940, he wrote two operas. All his work was published by the prestigious Schott publishing house in Mainz, Germany.

5 Gelasio Caetani (1877–1934) was another family polymath, able to turn his hand to sculpture and engineering as much as to works of conservation. He was a fine soldier and diplomat, and was Italian Ambassador to Washington

from 1922 to the end of 1924, overlapping with Esme Howard's ambassador-ship during that year.

6   *Theatre of Life*, i, 77–8.

7   Ibid.

8   Sir D'Arcy Osborne (1884–1964), later 12th Duke of Leeds, was British emissary to the Holy See from 1936 to 1947. He spent most of World War II inside the Vatican, where he helped protect some 4,000 Jews and Allied soldiers who had escaped the Nazis. His friend, Harold Tittmann Jr (1893–1980), kept a record of his wartime experience in Rome which his son later completed. It was published as *Inside the Vatican of Pius XII: The Memoir of an American Diplomat During World War II* (Doubleday, 2004).

9   Hubert's letter to Lelia, 21 December 1945, is cited courtesy of the CCF.

10 Ronald Knox (1888–1957) was a convert to the Catholic faith, an outstanding classicist (he translated the New Testament), and author. He was Catholic chaplain to Oxford University from 1926 to 1939 and Evelyn Waugh, one of England's most acclaimed twentieth-century novelists, wrote his biography (*Ronald Knox*, Chapman & Hall, 1959). Ironically, Lelia lost her ring in the sea at Sabaudia a decade after her wedding to Hubert. Shortly after the incident, she and Hubert visited Florence, staying with the Blue Nuns at Fiesole. As they checked in, Lelia expressed her humorous concern that the nuns might take her for an unmarried woman.

11 Tetton House, Somerset, dates from 1790 and was enlarged and mainly rebuilt in 1924–6 by the Hon. Mervyn Herbert (1882–1929). Mervyn's mother was Elizabeth 'Elsie' Carnarvon, Hubert's aunt and sister of his father Esme Howard.

12 *Domus Caietana*, originally published by the Fratelli Stianti in 1927, is now viewable on the CCF website at: <https://www.fondazionecamillocaetani.it/volumi-di-gelasio/>.

13 Exiled for opposing Boniface VIII's stance on papal supremacy as set out in the bull *Unam Sanctam* of 1302, Dante Alighieri, in his *Divine Comedy* of 1308, placed Boniface among the 'greedy popes and cardinals' in the fourth Circle of Hell. Worth noting here that the anti-clerical Michelangelo Caetani (1804–82), 13th Duke of Sermoneta, was a renowned Dante scholar. Reputedly, he could recite the entire *Divine Comedy* from memory.

14 The two Caetani cardinals cited, Niccolò (1526–85) and Enrico (1550–99), appear in portraits in the present day *salone* of the old municipal building or villa at Ninfa. Niccolò attempted, in the 1560s, to create his own garden in the then 150-years-old ruins of Ninfa. It is the garden still known today as the *Hortus Conclusus*, or walled garden, which retains various of the original features such as the sun dial.

15 At Lepanto, Onorato Caetani was aboard *La Grifona*, the first Christian vessel to come under attack by the Turks. On his triumphant return to

Sermoneta and to his wife Agnesina Colonna, sister of the admiral of the Spanish pontifical fleet, Onorato built the church of Santa Maria della Vittoria in thanksgiving. His marriage to a Colonna was another effort to reconcile the two families after so much mutual animosity.

16 The two dukes, both named Francesco, and living a century apart, worked against prevailing odds primarily to restore some economic value to the abandoned Ninfa. The second of them made a more enduring impact, with his various works of reconstruction and repair.

17 Cited in *Origine dell'antichissima e nobilissima Casa Caetani con li suoi Stati che possiede* (1911, facs. edn, *Quaderni di Ninfa*, Documenti, 1, RCF, 2011). Translation to English by the author.

18 Hubert's letter to Lelia, dated 24 March 1952, is quoted courtesy of the CCF.

19 Marguerite Caetani's *Botteghe Oscure*, described by her biographer Laurie Dennett (see Note 21 below) as a 'discerning and distinguished selection of international writing', encompassed a formidable array of writers of the mid-twentieth century, among them Dylan Thomas, Stephen Spender, Tennessee Williams, Truman Capote, Carlo Levi, Giorgio Bassani (see Note 22 below), Italo Calvino, Philippe Jaccottet, Albert Camus and René Char.

20 Benedetta Origo's account appears in the 2019 newsletter of the International Friends of Ninfa.

21 Les Amis de l'Art Contemporain was founded by Alice Warder Garrett, wife of John Garrett, American Ambassador to Italy from 1929 to 1933. Marguerite and Alice Garrett were joint vice-presidents of Les Amis, and provided most of the money. In Italy, there now exist a number of so-called literary parks, associated with individual men and women who have left their mark in the literary field. In 2019, Ninfa was awarded the status of literary park in honour of Marguerite Caetani. To all that had been written about Marguerite's life and work was added, in 2016, Laurie Dennett's fine biography, *An American Princess: The Remarkable Life of Marguerite Chapin Caetani* (McGill-Queen's University Press, 2016); translated into Italian by Lorenzo Salvagni, as *La Principessa Italiana* (Allemandi, 2020).

22 Giorgio Bassani (1916–2000), co-editor of *Botteghe Oscure*, was one of Italy's most revered scholars and novelists. In 2002, two years after his death, the Giorgio Bassani Foundation was established by his daughter Prof.ssa Paola Bassani, to honour and keep alive his memory.

23 The Camillo Caetani Foundation (CCF): <https://www.fondazionecamillocaetani.it>.

24 Elizabeth Jennings (1926–2001) ranks among the finest British poets of the second half of the twentieth century and is seen as the outstanding Catholic poet since Gerard Manley Hopkins. The poem 'Landscape and Wild Gardens' appears in *The Collected Poems* (Carcanet, 2012) and permission to quote from it is by courtesy of Messrs David Higham.

25 The Catholic Action movement, which is to be found in many countries, was established by Pope Pius X in Italy in 1905 as a non-political lay organization under the direct control of the bishops. A similar organization, Opera dei Congressi, was disbanded in 1904 by the same pope because many of its members were siding with modernism. Maria Teresa Cerocchi, Riccardo's wife, certainly exemplified her Gospel-based principles through her kindness and friendship to Hubert after he was widowed.

26 Among the first musicians to perform at the Caetani Castle in the early 1960s, with Lelia's permission and advocacy, were Yehudi Menuhin, Nikita Magaloff and Jacqueline du Pré. Today, the six-week Pontine Music Festival incorporates a student masterclass programme, and works in close association with the RCF.

27 Dominic Howard, one of Hubert's elder great-nephews (b. 1964). Like his brothers, sister and cousins, he stayed frequently as guest of Hubert and Lelia, over many years, at Ninfa and at Lyulph's Tower.

28 Giacomo Antonelli's anecdote appears in his introduction to the limited-edition anniversary publication *Lelia Caetani, Hubert Howard* (CCF, May 2007).

29 The great Christian Democrat statesman, Aldo Moro (1916–78), was murdered by the Red Brigades in May 1978, and his body dumped in the Via Michelangelo Caetani in Rome, abutting Palazzo Caetani. Moro had made a happy visit to Ninfa during his first term of office as prime minister of Italy. There is no sign of him in the Ninfa guest book but it was probably in summer 1968, and it had fallen to Mondi Howard, on a holiday visit from Genoa while serving there as British Consul General, to accompany him around the garden in Hubert and Lelia's absence. Mondi found Moro charming and appreciative, and was upset by his fate – no less so than by the wave of ungrounded political conspiracy theories which sections of the Italian press continued to circulate and to embellish, even after Hubert's death in 1987.

CHAPTER EIGHT: A CONSERVATIONIST AT HEART

1 These four co-founder members of Italia Nostra became close friends of Marguerite, Lelia and Hubert. Umberto Zanotti Bianco (1889–1963), esteemed patriot, philanthropist, archaeologist and environmentalist, became first chairman. As described in Chapter 7, the writer and intellectual Georgio Bassani (1916–2000) was particularly associated with Marguerite Caetani's review *Botteghe Oscure*, and he chaired Italia Nostra from 1965 to 1980. Desideria Pasolini dall'Onda (b. 1920), from an illustrious aristocratic Catholic family, has dedicated her life to the administration and management of the Pasolini properties. In the 1950s, with her degree in English from

Rome University, she helped Marguerite Caetani with *Botteghe Oscure*, going on to chair Italia Nostra from 1998 to 2005. Elena Croce (1915–94), eldest daughter of the intellectual and antifascist, Benedetto Croce, became a well-known writer, translator and environmentalist. In 1937 she married Raimondo Craveri (1912–92), himself a distinguished writer who also figured prominently in anti-fascist activity during the war.

2 The first Minutes of Italia Nostra are made available by courtesy of the association's Latina offices. On Italia Nostra's sixtieth anniversary, 23 November 2017, a well-attended ceremony took place at Ninfa, at which the Latina branch of the association adopted the name of Hubert Howard.

3 Charles Quest-Ritson, *Ninfa: The Most Romantic Garden in the World* (Frances Lincoln, 2009), 71.

4 Hubert's address, 'Per la Natura', was printed by the RFC in February 1989, on the second anniversary of his death, complete with a moving personal introduction by his friend Alessandro Onorati.

5 Lennart Bernadotte (1909–2004), Count of Wisborg, was born Prince Lennart, Duke of Småland. He was a grandson of King Gustaf V of Sweden. Insel Mainau is an inherited property which he developed into a tourist magnet, which, in spite of Hubert's distaste for certain aspects of it, enjoys reputable international links including ones with Kew Gardens, London.

6 Giuseppe Tomassetti (1848–1911), distinguished historian of the Middle Ages, was principally known for this work, an exhaustive study of the Roman countryside's history and topography. He began it in 1879, and it was concluded by his son Francesco who was responsible for the two volumes presented at Palazzo Caetani by Italia Nostra. The first volumes of *La Campagna Romana* were published from 1910.

7 Hubert's words are here translated by the author.

8 Charles V (1500–58) was Holy Roman Emperor and Archduke of Austria from 1519 to 1556, King of Spain (Castile and Aragon) from 1516 to 1556, and Lord of the Netherlands from 1506 to 1555.

9 Augustus Hare (1834–1903) was born in Rome, although educated in England. Author of many works, he is well known for his travel books, of which his two-volume *Walks in Rome* was first published by Strahan in 1872.

10 Published texts of the conference are among Hubert's papers/HFA.

CHAPTER NINE: THE FINAL YEARS

1 Hubert's February 1977 letters to his brothers, Mondi and Henry, following Lelia's death/HFA.

2 The late Giacomo Antonelli, married to a daughter of the prominent anti-fascist Nicolò Carandini and his author wife Elena (née Albertini), served as

lawyer to the Caetani family in Rome for many years. The architect Riccardo
Cerocchi raised his family in Latina. By the time he met Hubert and Lelia, he
already had an important role in the promotion of music in the Province of
Latina, where the seeds of the annual Pontine Music Festival had first been
planted by Hubert and Lelia in 1963, at the Caetani Castle. The International
Music Campus, part of the festival, was founded by Cerocchi in 1970, and
each year hosts a select body of mature students and internationally known
professors and performers. It operates in close association with the RCF and
is represented on its council.

3 From the 25 November 1978 minutes of the RCF, made available by courtesy
of the foundation. Of the first councillors, Fulco Pratesi would go on to
become president and later honorary president of the WWF in Italy, while
Arturo Osio would head up the National Park of the Stelvio in northern
Italy and in 1998 become chair of the RCF itself. In the 1980s, Paolo and
Laura Mora were instrumental in the restoration of the tomb of Nefertari
(favourite of the wives of Ramses II) in Luxor, Egypt. Over time, the RCF
would formalise the presence on the council, by right, of other conservational
associations, notable among them the Italian Fund for the Environment
(FAI) which has the same role and status in Italy as the National Trust in
England, Wales and Northern Ireland.

4 Hubert's letter to Francis, dated 5 November 1979/HFA.

5 Even in the eighteenth century, the fifteenth-century Caetani Codex of
Dante's *Divine Comedy* was well known to Dante scholars as one of the most
important manuscripts in the archive. It vanished inexplicably somewhere
in the palazzo during World War II. Through Hubert's initiative it was
rediscovered in 1976, and was the subject of a conference at the palazzo
in November 1979, highlighting annotations or glosses by the humanist
priest-scholar Marsilio Ficino (1433–99). The key speaker was Professor Paul
Oskar Kristeller of Columbia University in New York. The content of the
conference was reproduced in March 1981 to form Quaderno III of the CCF.

6 Kathleen Raine (1908–2003), one of Britain's foremost poets and educators,
achieved many honours. She was an almost exact contemporary of Hubert
and during World War II she lived for a while in Penrith, Cumbria. She
visited Ninfa many times and became a close friend of Hubert's. She was
inspired there to write her poem 'Ninfa Revisited', which has several times
been reproduced by the RCF. In 1981, under the patronage of the Prince of
Wales, she co-founded the Temenos Academy. Its work is dedicated to the
learning of the imagination and the perennial philosophy. It publishes an
annual review.

7 Had he lived, Hubert would greatly have appreciated another family
gathering that took place in 1994, at which Miles, 17th Duke of Norfolk,
a great unifier of the family, invited a large party of Howards to Rome to

pay respects to the two Howard cardinals, Philip and Edward, who lived respectively in the eighteenth and nineteenth centuries and did so much to conserve and develop the Venerable English College. After the Rome ceremonies honouring the two cardinals, the duke's entire party paid a visit to Ninfa, where they had lunch in the time-honoured tradition. The Norfolk Howards maintain their ties with the garden to this day.

8   This account is by courtesy of Fulco Pratesi, friend and colleague of Hubert and distinguished Italian conservationist.

9   Hubert's letter to Francis, dated 3 May 1981, regarding Ninfa activities/HFA.

10   Hubert's letter to Francis, dated 8 January 1983, regarding Rougemont and President Pertini's visit to Ninfa/HFA.

11   This story is by courtesy of Clotilde Luchetti. A lawyer, she currently serves on the council of the RCF, as did her late mother Gabriella Luchetti.

12   This walk up the Semprevisa is described in Hubert's letter to Mondi and Cécile Howard, dated 7 June 1983/HFA.

13   Fireblight is a bacterial disease that kills the shoots of apples, pears and related ornamentals, giving the plant the appearance of having been scorched by fire.

14   Hubert's letter to Francis, dated 21 April 1985, regarding the Prince and Princess of Wales' visit to Ninfa/HFA.

15   Hubert's letter to Francis, of 15 October 1986, saying he is not worried about the news of his terminal illness/HFA.

16   Fr John Dalrymple (1928–85) was author of a number of spiritual classics, among them *Letting Go in Love: Reflections on Spiritual Formation* (Darton, Longman and Todd, 1986).

17   Hubert's brother, Mondi, made detailed diary records of his stay in Rome before Christmas 1986/HFA.

18   Cardinal Edward Howard (1829–82) became a close advisor to Pope Pius IX and worked also with his successor Leo XIII. On 12 May 1879, a piece of history was made in his apartment at Palazzo Pigna, Rome. Here, John Henry Newman (1801–90) received the pope's *biglietto* appointing him cardinal, and made his famous acceptance speech.

19   Thetis Blacker (1927–2006) was a close friend of Kathleen Raine and a distinguished artist whose batik paintings can be seen in so many cathedrals of Europe, and in the United States. She visited Ninfa several times with Raine towards the end of Hubert's life. She was a Churchill Fellow and member of the Temenos Academy founded by Raine (see Note 6 above). Her farewell letter to Hubert is dated 15 December 1986. With it she enclosed her poem 'The Place' which she wrote while staying at Ninfa in May 1986. Her letter of condolence to Mondi is dated 7 March 1987/HFA.

20 Blaise Pascal (1623–62) was a mathematician and Christian philosopher of great distinction. His *Prayer to Ask of God the Proper Use of Sickness* is one of many of his reflections on suffering, which he felt to be the hallmark of the Christian life.

21 Malcolm Munthe's letter to Hubert, 2 February 1987/HFA.

22 Dame Iris Origo's description of Hubert's funeral service in Santa Maria in Campitelli, on 18 February 1987, and her personal tribute to Hubert, appeared in several newspapers at the time.

23 Fr John ('Jocky') Dalrymple is a parish priest, based now in Scotland. He is a nephew of Fr John Dalrymple (see Note 16 above).

24 Tessa Bennett's letter of condolence to Mondi, 17 February 1987/HFA.

25 Kathleen Raine's letter of condolence to Mondi, 17 February 1987/HFA.

26 Sir Paul Wright's letter of condolence to Mondi, 19 February 1987/HFA.

27 Abbot Aelred Sillem's letter of condolence to Mondi, 28 February 1987/ HFA.

28 Adam Munthe is the son of Malcolm Munthe (see Note 21 above and Note 16 to Chapter 5). He administers his family properties in England, offering to the public fine gardens and cultural activities. Munthe is a member of the Executive Committee of the International Friends of Ninfa, and his wife Nelly, née Rothschild, is an art restorer and one of the earliest nominees to the general council of the RCF.

29 James Lees-Milne's letter of condolence to Mondi, 28 February 1987/HFA.

30 Oliver Impy's letter of condolence to Mondi, c. 20 February 1987/HFA.

31 George Marylski's letter of condolence to Mondi, 17 February 1987/HFA.

32 James Clement Dunn (1890–1979) served as American Ambassador to Rome from 1946 to 1952. He continued to keep an apartment at Palazzo Caetani beyond his retirement in 1956.

33 Florence Hammond's letter to Hubert, 27 February 1987/HFA.

34 John Vernon's letter of condolence to Mondi, 23 February 1987/HFA.

Select Sources

HOWARD FAMILY ARCHIVES

Hubert Howard's personal correspondence from:

Downside, Cambridge and the US
Finland and wartime Italy
Rome and Ninfa during the period 1951 to 1987

Hubert's wartime files, diaries and other writings

PUBLICATIONS AND ARCHIVES OF THE CAMILLO CAETANI AND ROFFREDO CAETANI FOUNDATIONS

BIBLIOGRAPHY AND GENERAL REFERENCE

Anonymous, *The Life of Saint Philip Howard*, ed. Francis Steer (Phillimore, 1971)

Justin Brooke, *The Volunteers: The Full Story of the British Volunteers in Finland, 1939–41* (The Self-Publishing Association, 1990)

Jesse Childs, *Henry VIII's Last Victim: The Life and Times of Henry Howard, Earl of Surrey* (Jonathan Cape, 2006)

Laurie Dennett, *An American Princess: The Remarkable Life of Marguerite Chapin Caetani* (McGill-Queen's University Press, 2016)

Christopher Hibbert, *Florence: The Biography of a City* (Viking, 1993)

Esme Howard, *Virtues and Vanities* (MPG Books, 2012)

Lord Howard of Penrith, *Theatre of Life*, 2 vols. (Hodder & Stoughton, 1935–6)

Robert Hutchinson, *House of Treason* (Orion, 2009)

B. J. C. McKercher, *Esme Howard: A Diplomatic Biography* (Cambridge University Press, 1989)

Charles Quest-Ritson, *Ninfa: The Most Romantic Garden in the World* (Frances Lincoln, 2009)

John Martin Robinson, *The Dukes of Norfolk: A Quincentennial History* (Oxford University Press, 1982)

Gervase Vernon, *Love Letters in a Time of War* (Independently published, 2020)

Neville Williams, *Thomas Howard: Fourth Duke of Norfolk* (Barrie and Rockliff, 1964)

Picture Credits

Every effort has been made to identify, credit, and obtain publication rights from copyright holders of illustrations in this book. Notice of any errors or omissions in this regard will be gratefully received and corrections will be made in any subsequent editions. All unspecified attributions are to the Howard Family Archives (HFA).

The following images are by courtesy of:

> *The Duke of Norfolk*   pages 22, 25
> *Archivio Masogiba*   page 29
> *Chronicle/Alamy Stock Photo*   page 51
> *Finnish Defence Forces/SA-kuva*   page 60
> *Camillo Caetani Foundation*   pages 84–6, 88, 99
> *Greymouser/Wikimedia Commons*   page 95
> *Bain Collection/Library of Congress*   page 97
> *Carlotta Lowe*   page 152
> *Roffredo Caetani Foundation*   page 153

PLATES

Coat of arms of the Howard Dukes of Norfolk; Thomas Howard, 3rd Duke of Norfolk; Thomas Howard, 4th Duke of Norfolk; St Philip Howard, Earl of Arundel   *from the archives of Arundel Castle, by courtesy of the Duke of Norfolk* ✦ Esme Howard's tapestry; Lelia's painting of Hubert   *by courtesy of the Roffredo Caetani Foundation* ✦ Ullswater viewed from above Lyulph's Tower   *by courtesy of Michelle Kacich* ✦ Castle of Lanciano; Salone Antinori   *by courtesy of the Archivio Masogiba. Publication authorised by the chairman of Ma.So.Gi.Ba, Avv. Luigi Tapanelli* ✦ Esme, Lord Howard of Penrith, by Henry Harris Brown   *by courtesy of Lord Howard of Penrith* ✦ André Derain's portrait of Lelia   *by courtesy of the Camillo Caetani Foundation*

Index

Index